Contents

12

52

68

*D*uring the holiday season, parties and family gatherings are all about spending time with the people you love. Whatever holiday you celebrate, food plays an important role in many gatherings.

Most people love to reconnect with family and friends, and planning and preparing the special treats for holiday gatherings provides the opportunity to nurture these special connections. With this in mind, the special food ideas in this booklet can be quickly and easily prepared using familiar ingredients, along with your favorite **NABISCO** Crackers. In *Celebration Starters, Mix 'n Mingle Dips & Spreads,* and *Crowd-Pleasing Cracker Toppings*, you'll find a wide range of easy-to-prepare hearty appetizers, snacks, dips, and spreads. Not only will they satisfy your guests, but they'll also ensure that you won't miss the party yourself! We start with the great flavor and crunch of **TRISCUIT** Crackers, made with 100% whole grains and zero trans fat, **RITZ** Crackers, with their buttery, melt-in-your-mouth flavor and flaky crunch, and the multi-dimensional flavor of **WHEAT THINS** Snack Crackers. Their shapes, flavors, and textures complement the creamy and savory selection of dips, spreads, and toppings perfectly. Furthermore, if looking for better-for-you options, check the nutrition information to find recipes that meet your goals.

We have included some show-stopping desserts in *Tasteful Traditions*, along with simple tips for presenting your food with style and pizzazz. With the goodness of **NILLA** Wafers, **OREO** Chocolate Sandwich Cookies, and **HONEY MAID** Honey Grahams, these wonderful family pleasers are deliciously simple. They're perfect for parties since they can be assembled ahead of time and decorated just before serving. Lastly, *Gift-Giving Favorites* is dedicated to the creation of homemade gifts from your very own kitchen. We hope that you enjoy preparing these as much as we enjoyed creating them for you and your family.

As you plan ahead for the holiday season, these recipes can help you entertain with a savvy, sophisticated style while you create lasting memories and have fun at your own parties!

Marianne Arimenta-Dente
Kraft Kitchens

CELEBRATION

**Extra-special appetizers for those
extra-special holiday gatherings**

STARTERS

SHRIMP SPREAD

Prep: 15 min. ● Total: 15 min.

- **1** lb. frozen peeled and deveined shrimp **(41 to 50 count)**, cooked, divided
- **1** pkg. (8 oz.) **PHILADELPHIA** Cream Cheese, softened
- **¾** cup finely chopped celery
- **¼** cup finely chopped stuffed green olives

    RITZ Crackers

CHOP enough shrimp to measure 1 cup; place in medium bowl. Set remaining shrimp aside for later use.

ADD cream cheese, celery and olives to shrimp in bowl; mix well. Spoon onto center of serving plate. Shape into 6-inch round. Arrange remaining shrimp around edge of cream cheese mixture, pressing gently into cream cheese mixture to secure.

SERVE with crackers.

Makes 16 servings, 2 Tbsp. spread and 5 crackers each.

Nutrition Information Per Serving: 160 calories, 10g total fat, 4g saturated fat, 310mg sodium, 11g carbohydrate, 8g protein.

How to Devein Raw Shrimp:

To devein raw shrimp, remove the outer shell first. Then make a lengthwise shallow cut on the outer curve of the shrimp. (This will expose the black vein.) Loosen the vein with the tip of a sharp knife and then pull with your fingers to completely remove.

SOUTHERN-STYLE CRAB CAKES WITH COOL LIME SAUCE

Prep: 15 min. ● Total: 23 min.

Grated peel and juice from 1 lime, divided

1 cup **KRAFT** Mayo Real Mayonnaise or **MIRACLE WHIP** Dressing, divided

1 env. **GOOD SEASONS** Italian Salad Dressing & Recipe Mix

2 Tbsp. **GREY POUPON** Country Dijon Mustard

2 cans (6 oz. each) crabmeat, drained, flaked

25 **RITZ** Crackers, finely crushed, divided

1 green onion, chopped

¼ cup **BREAKSTONE'S** or **KNUDSEN** Sour Cream

MIX half of the lime juice, ½ cup of the mayo, the salad dressing mix and mustard in medium bowl until well blended. Add crabmeat, ½ cup of the cracker crumbs and the onion; mix lightly.

SHAPE into 18 (½-inch-thick) patties; coat with remaining cracker crumbs.

COOK patties in batches in large nonstick skillet on medium heat 2 min. on each side or until browned on both sides and heated through. Meanwhile, mix remaining ½ cup mayo, remaining lime juice, the lime peel and sour cream until well blended. Serve with crab cakes.

Makes 18 servings, 1 crab cake and 2 tsp. sauce each.

Note: If skillet is not nonstick, cook crab cakes in 1 Tbsp. oil.

Nutrition Information Per Serving: 140 calories, 12g total fat, 2g saturated fat, 340mg sodium, 4g carbohydrate, 4g protein.

Jazz It Up:

Spoon sauce decoratively onto serving plate before topping with crab cakes. Garnish with a lime slice and additional chopped green onions.

ROASTED RED PEPPER-BASIL SPREAD

Prep: 15 min. ● Total: 1 hour 15 min. (incl. refrigerating)

1 tub (12 oz.) **PHILADELPHIA** Cream Cheese Spread

¼ cup lightly packed fresh basil leaves

1 clove garlic, peeled

¼ cup drained roasted red peppers

5 pitted black olives, chopped

2 Tbsp. **PLANTERS** Sliced Almonds, toasted

RITZ Crackers

PLACE cream cheese spread in blender; set aside. Wash tub; line with plastic wrap, with ends of wrap extending over side of tub. Set aside.

ADD basil and garlic to cream cheese in blender; cover. Blend using pulsing action until well blended; set aside. Cut a star shape from one of the peppers, using ½-inch star-shaped cutter; set star aside for later use. Chop pepper trimmings and remaining peppers; combine with the olives. Spoon ½ cup of the cream cheese mixture into prepared tub. Cover with the chopped pepper mixture; press lightly into cream cheese mixture. Top with the remaining cream cheese mixture; cover. Refrigerate 1 hour.

UNMOLD cheese spread onto serving plate; remove and discard plastic wrap. Top cheese spread with the almonds and pepper star. Serve as a spread with the crackers.

Makes 1½ cups or 12 servings, 2 Tbsp. spread and 5 crackers each.

Make Ahead: Prepare cheese spread as directed. Cover and refrigerate up to 24 hours. Unmold and continue as directed.

Nutrition Information Per Serving: 180 calories, 13g total fat, 6g saturated fat, 300mg sodium, 12g carbohydrate, 3g protein.

Jazz It Up:

For a holiday flair, serve with RITZ SIMPLY SOCIALS Crackers.

EASY RITZ HOT WINGS

Prep: 20 min. ● Total: 1 hour

1 sleeve **RITZ** Crackers (38 crackers), finely crushed

1 tsp. dried oregano leaves

½ tsp. garlic powder

½ tsp. paprika

⅛ tsp. coarsely ground black pepper

2 lb. chicken wings, separated at joints, tips discarded

½ cup hot pepper sauce

PREHEAT oven to 350°F. Mix cracker crumbs and seasonings in shallow dish.

COAT chicken with hot pepper sauce, then dip in crumb mixture, turning to evenly coat both sides of each wing piece. Place in single layer on greased baking sheet.

BAKE 35 to 40 min. or until golden brown and cooked through (165°F), turning pieces over after 20 min. Serve warm.

Makes 20 servings, about 1 chicken wing each.

Nutrition Information Per Serving: 120 calories, 7g total fat, 2g saturated fat, 160mg sodium, 4g carbohydrate, 8g protein.

Serving Suggestion:

Serve these flavorful appetizers with vegetable sticks and KRAFT ROKA Blue Cheese Dressing.

CRANBERRY AND PECAN CHEESE LOG

Prep: 15 min. ● Total: 45 min. (incl. refrigerating)

1 container (8 oz.) **PHILADELPHIA** Light Cream Cheese Spread

¼ cup chopped dried cranberries

1 Tbsp. grated orange peel

½ cup coarsely chopped **PLANTERS** Pecans, toasted

TRISCUIT Rosemary & Olive Oil Crackers

MIX cream cheese spread, cranberries and orange peel until well blended. Shape into 6-inch log.

ROLL in pecans until evenly coated on all sides. Wrap tightly in plastic wrap.

REFRIGERATE at least 30 min. Serve as a spread with the crackers.

Makes 1½ cups or 12 servings, 2 Tbsp. spread and 6 crackers each.

Nutrition Information Per Serving: 200 calories, 10g total fat, 2.5g saturated fat, 220mg sodium, 24g carbohydrate, 5g protein.

Take Along:

Bringing this colorful cheese log to a holiday party? Remember to pack a copy of the recipe. You're sure to get requests!

SHALLOT & BACON BRIE

Prep: 10 min. ● Total: 11 min.

2 slices **OSCAR MAYER** Bacon

2 shallots, thinly sliced

2 tsp. **GREY POUPON** Savory Honey Mustard

1 wheel Brie cheese (8 oz.)

RITZ Crackers

COOK bacon in nonstick skillet on medium heat until crisp. Drain bacon, reserving drippings in skillet; set bacon aside.

ADD shallots to bacon drippings in skillet; cook until shallots are tender, stirring frequently. Crumble bacon into small bowl. Add shallot mixture and mustard; mix well. Spoon over cheese in microwaveable serving dish.

MICROWAVE on HIGH 45 sec. or just until cheese is warmed. Serve as a spread with the crackers.

Makes 16 servings, 2 Tbsp. spread and 5 crackers each.

Nutrition Information Per Serving: 150 calories, 10g total fat, 4g saturated fat, 270mg sodium, 12g carbohydrate, 5g protein.

The Perfect Cheese Tray:

Cheese trays are ideal for entertaining. Be sure to include a selection of KRAFT Cheeses in mild, medium and strong flavors. Cut cheeses into an assortment of shapes, then arrange on a large tray or platter along with a sampling of NABISCO Crackers and colorful fresh fruit.

THE ULTIMATE STUFFED MUSHROOM

Prep: 20 min. ● Total: 35 min.

20 mushrooms

3 Tbsp. butter

2 Tbsp. finely chopped onions

2 Tbsp. finely chopped red peppers

14 **RITZ** Crackers, finely crushed (about ½ cup crumbs)

2 Tbsp. **KRAFT** 100% Grated Parmesan Cheese

½ tsp. Italian seasoning

PREHEAT oven to 400°F. Remove stems from mushrooms. Finely chop enough of the stems to measure ¼ cup; set aside. Cover and refrigerate remaining stems for other use.

MELT butter in large skillet on medium heat. Add ¼ cup chopped mushroom stems, the onions and peppers; cook and stir until vegetables are tender. Stir in cracker crumbs, cheese and Italian seasoning. Spoon crumb mixture evenly into mushroom caps. Place on baking sheet.

BAKE 15 min. or until heated through.

Makes 20 servings, 1 stuffed mushroom each.

Make Ahead: Mushrooms can be stuffed several hours in advance. Cover and refrigerate until ready to serve. Uncover and bake at 400°F for 20 min. or until heated through.

Nutrition Information Per Serving: 35 calories, 2.5g total fat, 1g saturated fat, 45mg sodium, 2g carbohydrate, 1g protein.

Make It Easy:

When preparing mushrooms for stuffing, use a melon baller to carefully scoop a little mushroom flesh from the cap after removing the stem. Then use the melon baller to easily scoop the filling mixture into the mushrooms.

ROASTED EGGPLANT CAPONATA

Prep: 1 hour 10 min. ● Total: 3 hours 10 min. (incl. refrigerating)

1 **head garlic**

1 **Tbsp. olive oil**

1 **large eggplant (1½ lb.)**

1 **can (14½ oz.) diced tomatoes, drained**

¼ **cup chopped fresh parsley**

2 **Tbsp. chopped red onions**

2 **Tbsp. balsamic vinegar**

¼ **tsp. salt**

1 **Tbsp. KRAFT Shredded Parmesan Cheese**

WHEAT THINS Snack Crackers

PREHEAT oven to 375°F. Cut ½-inch-thick slice off top of garlic, exposing cloves; discard top. Brush cut-side of garlic lightly with oil; wrap tightly in foil. Place on ungreased baking sheet. Pierce eggplant in several places with fork or sharp knife. Place on baking sheet with garlic. Bake 50 min. to 1 hour or until both are tender; cool slightly.

PEEL eggplant; cut into small pieces. Place in medium bowl. Mince 3 of the garlic cloves. Add to eggplant along with the tomatoes, parsley, onions, vinegar and salt; mix well. Cover; refrigerate at least 2 hours. Meanwhile, store remaining garlic in refrigerator for another use.

SPRINKLE eggplant mixture with cheese just before serving. Serve as a dip with the crackers.

Makes 2 cups or 16 servings, 2 Tbsp. dip and 16 crackers each.

How to Serve Warm: Just before serving, spoon the dip into microwaveable bowl. Microwave on HIGH 1 min., stirring after 30 sec.

Nutrition Information Per Serving: 170 calories, 7g total fat, 1g saturated fat, 320mg sodium, 24g carbohydrate, 3g protein.

Creative Leftovers:

Store leftover roasted garlic in tightly covered container in refrigerator. Spread onto your favorite NABISCO Crackers, then top with any leftover eggplant mixture.

MARINATED FETA CHEESE

Prep: 10 min. ● Total: 1 hour 10 min. (incl. refrigerating)

1 pkg. (8 oz.) **ATHENOS** Traditional Feta Cheese

2 Tbsp. **GOOD SEASONS** Italian Vinaigrette with Extra Virgin Olive Oil Dressing

1 tsp. finely chopped fennel tops

1 tsp. finely chopped fresh rosemary

¼ tsp. crushed red pepper

¼ tsp. grated lemon peel

CUT cheese into 32 cubes; place in medium bowl.

ADD remaining ingredients; mix lightly. Cover.

REFRIGERATE at least 1 hour.

Makes 8 servings, 4 cheese cubes each.

Make Ahead: Cheese mixture can be refrigerated up to 24 hours before serving.

Nutrition Information Per Serving (cheese only): 80 calories, 7g total fat, 4.5g saturated fat, 360mg sodium, 1g carbohydrate, 5g protein.

Serving Suggestion:

Serve with SOCIABLES Savory Crackers, RITZ Snowflake Crackers or RITZ SIMPLY SOCIALS Crackers.

MIX 'N MINGLE

Make these recipes ahead of time and enjoy the party with your guests!

DIPS &

SPREADS

LAYERED PESTO AND RED PEPPER DIP

Prep: 15 min. ● Total: 1 hour 15 min.
(incl. refrigerating)

- 1 tub (8 oz.) **PHILADELPHIA** Light Cream Cheese Spread, divided
- ¼ cup chopped drained roasted red peppers
- 1 Tbsp. pesto
- 1 Tbsp. milk
- **WHEAT THINS** Snack Crackers

PLACE half of the cream cheese spread and the peppers in blender; cover. Blend 30 to 40 sec. or until well blended, stopping and scraping down side of blender as needed.

MIX remaining cream cheese spread, pesto and milk until well blended. Spread onto small serving plate; top with the red pepper mixture. Cover.

REFRIGERATE at least 1 hour before serving.

Makes about 1 cup or 9 servings, 2 Tbsp. dip and 16 crackers each.

Make Ahead: The 2 layers of dip can be made up to 1 day ahead and stored in separate tightly covered containers in the refrigerator. For best results, layer the dips no more than 2 hours before serving.

Nutrition Information Per Serving: 210 calories, 10g total fat, 3g saturated fat, 420mg sodium, 23g carbohydrate, 5g protein.

HOT APPLE PIE DIP

Prep: 10 min. ● Total: 22 min.

- **1 tub (8 oz.) PHILADELPHIA** Light Cream Cheese Spread
- **2 Tbsp.** brown sugar
- **½ tsp.** pumpkin pie spice
- **1** apple, chopped, divided
- **¼ cup KRAFT** 2% Milk Shredded Reduced Fat Cheddar Cheese
- **1 Tbsp.** finely chopped **PLANTERS** Pecan Pieces
- **WHEAT THINS** Lightly Cinnamon Snack Crackers

PREHEAT oven to 375°F. Mix cream cheese spread, sugar and spice in medium bowl until well blended. Stir in half of the chopped apple.

SPREAD into 8-inch pie plate or small casserole dish. Top with remaining apples, the Cheddar cheese and pecans.

BAKE 10 to 12 min. or until heated through. Serve with the crackers.

Makes 2 cups or 16 servings, 2 Tbsp. dip and 15 crackers each.

Substitute: Substitute ground cinnamon for the pumpkin pie spice.

Nutrition Information Per Serving: 190 calories, 8g total fat, 2.5g saturated fat, 210mg sodium, 25g carbohydrate, 4g protein.

LAYERED HOT ARTICHOKE AND FETA DIP

Prep: 10 min. ● Total: 30 min.

1 pkg. (8 oz.) **PHILADELPHIA** Neufchâtel Cheese, softened

1 can (14 oz.) artichoke hearts, drained, chopped

½ cup **KRAFT** Shredded Parmesan Cheese

2 cloves garlic, minced

1 small red pepper, chopped

1 pkg. (3.5 oz.) **ATHENOS** Crumbled Reduced Fat Feta Cheese

1 Tbsp. sliced black olives

   WHEAT THINS Toasted Chips Multi-Grain

PREHEAT oven to 350°F. Mix Neufchâtel, artichokes, Parmesan cheese and garlic until well blended.

SPREAD into 3-cup ovenproof serving dish; top with peppers and feta cheese.

BAKE 20 min.; top with olives. Serve with the chips.

Makes 3 cups or 24 servings, 2 Tbsp. dip and 15 chips each.

Make Ahead: Assemble dip as directed; cover and refrigerate up to 8 hours. When ready to serve, uncover and bake at 350°F for 25 min. or until heated through.

Nutrition Information Per Serving: 170 calories, 7g total fat, 2.5g saturated fat, 500mg sodium, 22g carbohydrate, 5g protein.

CHUNKY VEGETABLE HUMMUS

Prep: 10 min. ● Total: 10 min.

1 container (7 oz.) **ATHENOS** Original Hummus

¾ cup chopped, peeled and seeded cucumbers

¼ cup chopped red onions

1 plum tomato, chopped

¼ cup **ATHENOS** Traditional Crumbled Feta Cheese

WHEAT THINS Big Snack Crackers

SPREAD hummus onto serving plate.

TOP with layers of cucumbers, onions and tomatoes; sprinkle with cheese.

SERVE with the crackers.

Makes 2½ cups or 20 servings, 2 Tbsp. dip and 11 crackers each.

Substitute: Prepare as directed, using **ATHENOS** Crumbled Reduced Fat Feta Cheese.

Nutrition Information Per Serving: 170 calories, 7g total fat, 1.5g saturated fat, 350mg sodium, 24g carbohydrate, 3g protein.

Shortcut:

Save time by preparing with already-chopped vegetables purchased at the salad bar in your local supermarket.

CHEESY SPINACH AND ARTICHOKE DIP

Prep: 10 min. ● Total: 30 min.

1 can (14 oz.) artichoke hearts, drained, finely chopped

1 pkg. (10 oz.) frozen chopped spinach, thawed, drained

¾ cup **KRAFT** 100% Grated Parmesan Cheese

¾ cup **KRAFT** Mayo Light Mayonnaise

½ cup **KRAFT** 2% Milk Shredded Reduced Fat Mozzarella Cheese

½ tsp. garlic powder

WHEAT THINS Toasted Chips Multi-Grain

PREHEAT oven to 350°F. Mix all ingredients except chips until well blended.

SPOON into 9-inch pie plate or quiche dish.

BAKE 20 min. or until heated through. Serve with the chips.

Makes 2¾ cups or 22 servings, 2 Tbsp. dip and 15 chips each.

Nutrition Information Per Serving: 190 calories, 9g total fat, 2g saturated fat, 500mg sodium, 23g carbohydrate, 5g protein.

Variation:

Awesome Spinach and Mushroom Dip: Substitute 1 cup chopped mushrooms for the artichoke hearts.

PINECONE CHEESE SPREAD

Prep: 20 min. ● Total: 2 hours 35 min. (incl. refrigerating)

1 pkg. (8 oz.) **PHILADELPHIA** Cream Cheese, softened

1 pkg. (8 oz.) **KRAFT** 2% Milk Shredded Reduced Fat Four Cheese Mexican Style Cheese

2 Tbsp. **GREY POUPON** Dijon Mustard

2 Tbsp. chopped canned green chilies

⅓ cup **PLANTERS** Sliced Almonds, toasted

RITZ Crackers

PLACE cream cheese, shredded cheese and mustard in food processor or blender; cover. Process until well blended. Stir in chilies.

PLACE on sheet of waxed paper; shape into 4-inch oval to resemble a pinecone. Insert almonds in rows to completely cover cream cheese mixture; cover.

REFRIGERATE 2 hours or until firm. Let stand at room temperature 15 min. before serving with the crackers.

Makes 2 cups or 16 servings, 2 Tbsp. spread and 5 crackers each.

Make Ahead: Spread can be stored, tightly covered, in refrigerator up to 5 days.

Substitute: Serve with **RITZ** Snowflake Crackers.

Nutrition Information Per Serving: 190 calories, 13g total fat, 6g saturated fat, 360mg sodium, 11g carbohydrate, 6g protein.

Jazz It Up:

Prepare as directed, adding 1 tsp. hot pepper sauce to the cream cheese mixture before shaping as directed.

HOT HOLIDAY BROCCOLI DIP

Prep: 10 min. ● Total: 40 min.

1 cup MIRACLE WHIP Light Dressing

1 pkg. (10 oz.) frozen chopped broccoli, thawed, well drained

1 jar (2 oz.) diced pimientos, drained

½ cup KRAFT 100% Grated Parmesan Cheese

1 cup KRAFT 2% Milk Shredded Reduced Fat Mozzarella Cheese, divided

WHEAT THINS Snack Crackers

PREHEAT oven to 350°F. Combine dressing, broccoli, pimientos, Parmesan cheese and ½ cup of the mozzarella cheese.

SPREAD into baking dish or 9-inch pie plate.

BAKE 20 to 25 min. or until heated through. Sprinkle with remaining ½ cup mozzarella cheese. Bake an additional 5 min. or until mozzarella cheese is melted. Serve with the crackers.

Makes about 3 cups or 25 servings, about 2 Tbsp. dip and 16 crackers each.

Nutrition Information Per Serving: 180 calories, 8g total fat, 2g saturated fat, 440mg sodium, 23g carbohydrate, 5g protein.

Time-Out:

Take a time-out during the busy holiday season to watch a movie or two! Pick a holiday classic or something that's guaranteed to make you laugh. Prepare your favorite snack and enjoy!

CHEESY HOT CRAB AND RED PEPPER DIP

Prep: 10 min. ● Total: 30 min.

1½ cups **KRAFT** 2% Milk Shredded Reduced Fat Mozzarella Cheese, divided

1 pkg. (8 oz.) **PHILADELPHIA** Neufchâtel Cheese, softened

1 tsp. garlic powder

1 tsp. Italian seasoning

1 medium red pepper, chopped

1 small onion, finely chopped

1 can (6 oz.) crabmeat, drained

WHEAT THINS Snack Crackers

PREHEAT oven to 375°F. Remove ½ cup of the mozzarella cheese; cover and refrigerate until ready to use. Mix all remaining ingredients except crackers until well blended.

SPREAD into 9-inch pie plate.

BAKE 20 min. or until crab mixture is heated through and top is lightly browned. Sprinkle with reserved ½ cup mozzarella cheese. Serve hot with the crackers.

Makes 3 cups or 24 servings, 2 Tbsp. dip and 16 crackers each.

Substitute: Prepare as directed, using **PHILADELPHIA** Cream Cheese and **KRAFT** Shredded Mozzarella Cheese. Serve with **WHEAT THINS** Toasted Chips Multi-Grain or **RITZ** Toasted Chips.

Nutrition Information Per Serving: 200 calories, 9g total fat, 3g saturated fat, 380mg sodium, 22g carbohydrate, 7g protein.

APPLE, PECAN & BLUE CHEESE SPREAD

Prep: 10 min. ● Total: 2 hours 10 min. (incl. refrigerating)

1 container (8 oz.) **PHILADELPHIA** Light Cream Cheese Spread

½ cup **BREAKSTONE'S** Reduced Fat or **KNUDSEN** Light Sour Cream

1 Rome Beauty apple, finely chopped

¼ cup **ATHENOS** Crumbled Blue Cheese

¼ cup chopped red onion

¼ cup chopped toasted **PLANTERS** Pecans

TRISCUIT Crackers

BEAT cream cheese spread and sour cream in medium bowl until well blended.

ADD apples, blue cheese, onions and pecans; mix well. Cover.

REFRIGERATE at least 2 hours. Serve as a spread with the crackers.

Makes 3 cups or 24 servings, 2 Tbsp. spread and 6 crackers each.

Nutrition Information Per Serving: 170 calories, 8g total fat, 2.5g saturated fat, 250mg sodium, 22g carbohydrate, 4g protein.

Serving Suggestion:

For a unique dip container, cut top off and hollow out a large red apple. Stand upright on serving platter and fill with dip just before serving. Surround with crackers.

CHEESY CHRISTMAS TREE

Prep: 10 min. ● Total: 10 min.

1 pkg. (8 oz.) **PHILADELPHIA** Cream Cheese

1 stick **KRAFT POLLY-O TWIST-UMS** String Cheese

½ cup pesto

¼ cup chopped red peppers

　RITZ Crackers

CUT block of cream cheese diagonally in half. Arrange both halves, with points together, on serving plate to resemble Christmas-tree shape.

CUT a 2-inch piece from the string cheese. Place at bottom of tree for the trunk. Wrap up remaining string cheese; refrigerate until ready to use for snacking or other use.

SPOON pesto over cream cheese; sprinkle with peppers. Serve as a spread with the crackers.

Makes 1½ cups or 12 servings, 2 Tbsp. spread and 5 crackers each.

Substitute: Prepare as directed, using **PHILADELPHIA** Neufchâtel Cheese.

Nutrition Information Per Serving: 200 calories, 16g total fat, 6g saturated fat, 280mg sodium, 12g carbohydrate, 3g protein.

CROWD-PLEASING
CRACKER

Perfect pairings of crunchy crackers
and special toppings for
your most elegant gatherings

TOPPINGS

"BRUSCHETTA" TRISCUIT

Prep: 10 min. ● Total: 10 min.

- 1 small tomato, finely chopped (about ½ cup)
- ¼ cup **KRAFT** 2% Milk Shredded Reduced Fat Mozzarella Cheese
- 3 Tbsp. sliced green onions
- 1 Tbsp. **KRAFT** Light Zesty Italian Reduced Fat Dressing
- 40 **TRISCUIT** Crackers
- 1 pkg. (8 oz.) **PHILADELPHIA** Neufchâtel Cheese, softened

MIX tomatoes, cheese, onions and dressing.

SPREAD each cracker with about 1 tsp. of the Neufchâtel; top with 1 tsp. of the tomato mixture.

Makes 20 servings, 2 topped crackers each.

Make Ahead: Prepare tomato mixture as directed. Add Neufchâtel; mix well. Cover and refrigerate up to 24 hours. Spread onto crackers just before serving.

Nutrition Information Per Serving: 70 calories, 4.5g total fat, 2g saturated fat, 130mg sodium, 7g carbohydrate, 2g protein.

CAPRESE TOPPER

Prep: 5 min. ● Total: 12 min.

4 oz. **POLLY-O** Part Skim Mozzarella Cheese, cut into 9 slices

18 **TRISCUIT** Fire Roasted Tomato & Olive Oil Crackers

2 plum tomatoes, cut into 9 slices each

1 Tbsp. pesto

18 small fresh basil leaves

PREHEAT oven to 350°F. Cut each cheese slice in half.

TOP crackers with cheese and tomatoes. Place on baking sheet.

BAKE 5 to 7 min. or until cheese is melted. Top with pesto and basil. Serve warm.

Makes 1½ doz. or 9 servings, 2 topped crackers each.

Serving Suggestion: When serving appetizers, offer a variety of colors, shapes and flavors. Include an assortment of dips, cracker toppers and spreads in both hot and cold forms.

Nutrition Information Per Serving: 90 calories, 4.5g total fat, 2g saturated fat, 160mg sodium, 8g carbohydrate, 5g protein.

SHRIMP APPETIZERS WITH GREEN MAYONNAISE

Prep: 20 min. ● Total: 1 hour 20 min. (incl. refrigerating)

- ¼ cup **KRAFT** Mayo Light Mayonnaise
- 2 Tbsp. minced fresh parsley
- 1 Tbsp. finely chopped green onion
- ½ tsp. grated lime peel
- 18 shrimp (31 to 40 count), cleaned, cooked
- 18 **WHEAT THINS** Big Snack Crackers

MIX mayo, parsley, onion and lime peel in medium bowl. Add shrimp; toss to evenly coat. Cover.

REFRIGERATE at least 1 hour.

SPOON onto crackers just before serving.

Makes 1½ doz. or 6 servings, 3 topped crackers each.

Substitute: Prepare as directed, using **RITZ** Crackers or **TRISCUIT** Crackers.

Shrimp Sizes: The size of a shrimp is indicated by the number of shrimp per pound. The smaller the number, the larger the shrimp. Less than 15 is jumbo shrimp; 16 to 20 is extra-large shrimp; 21 to 30 is large shrimp; and 31 to 40 is medium shrimp.

Nutrition Information Per Serving (without garnish): 90 calories, 5g total fat, 1g saturated fat, 190mg sodium, 7g carbohydrate, 3g protein.

Jazz It Up:

Top each appetizer with small strips of roasted red peppers and a parsley sprig.

ARTICHOKE-CHEESE PUFFS

Prep: 10 min. ● Total: 50 min. (incl. refrigerating)

36 **RITZ** Crackers, divided

1 pkg. (8 oz.) **PHILADELPHIA** Cream Cheese, softened

¼ cup **KRAFT** 100% Grated Parmesan Cheese

¼ cup **KRAFT** 2% Milk Shredded Reduced Fat Mozzarella Cheese

½ cup chopped drained canned artichoke hearts

CRUSH 4 of the crackers. Place in shallow dish; set aside. Mix cheeses and artichokes until well blended. Shape 2 tsp. of the cheese mixture into ball. (If cheese mixture is too soft, cover and refrigerate until firm enough to shape into ball.) Repeat with remaining cheese mixture to make a total of 32 balls. Roll in cracker crumbs until evenly coated. Place in single layer on waxed paper-covered tray; cover. Refrigerate 30 min.

PREHEAT oven to 350°F. Arrange remaining 32 crackers in single layer on baking sheet; top each with 1 cheese ball.

BAKE 10 min. or until heated through.

Makes 16 servings, 2 cheese puffs each.

Shortcut: Serve these delicious appetizers cold. Prepare cheese balls as directed and refrigerate up to 24 hours. Place 1 cheese ball on each cracker just before serving.

Substitute: Prepare as directed, using **RITZ** Snowflake Crackers.

Nutrition Information Per Serving (with cracker crumb coating): 100 calories, 8g total fat, 4g saturated fat, 200mg sodium, 6g carbohydrate, 3g protein.

Jazz It Up:

Try adding one of the following to the cracker crumbs: toasted sesame seeds; chopped fresh dill or fresh chives; finely chopped red, green and yellow peppers. Or omit the crumbs and coat only in the alternative coating.

RED ONION-BALSAMIC TOPPER

Prep: 10 min. • Total: 52 min.

 1 Tbsp. olive oil

 1 red onion, thinly sliced (about 1 cup)

 2 Tbsp. balsamic vinegar

48 **TRISCUIT** Rosemary & Olive Oil Crackers

 ¼ cup **BREAKSTONE'S** Reduced Fat or **KNUDSEN** Light Sour Cream

HEAT oil in large skillet on medium heat. Add onions; cook 10 min. or until tender, stirring frequently. Stir in vinegar; cook an additional 1 to 2 min. or until vinegar is evaporated. Cool.

SPOON 1 tsp. of the onion mixture onto each cracker; top with ¼ tsp. of the sour cream.

SERVE warm.

Makes 4 doz. or 16 servings, 3 topped crackers each.

Creative Leftovers: For a heartier appetizer, top each cracker with a thin slice of leftover cooked steak before covering with the onion mixture and sour cream.

Nutrition Information Per Serving: 80 calories, 3.5g total fat, 0.5g saturated fat, 70mg sodium, 11g carbohydrate, 2g protein.

Jazz It Up:
Garnish topped crackers with chopped fresh parsley.

TUSCAN CHICKEN BITES

Prep: 15 min. ● Total: 1 hour 15 min. (incl. refrigerating)

1 small boneless, skinless chicken breast half (4 oz.), cooked, finely chopped (about ¾ cup)

¼ cup **BREAKSTONE'S FREE** or **KNUDSEN FREE** Fat Free Sour Cream

2 green onions, finely chopped

2 Tbsp. finely chopped roasted red peppers

1 tsp. grated lemon peel

½ tsp. chopped fresh rosemary

24 **TRISCUIT** Cracked Pepper & Olive Oil Crackers

24 baby arugula leaves

COMBINE all ingredients except crackers and arugula; cover.

REFRIGERATE at least 1 hour.

TOP each cracker with 1 arugula leaf and 2 tsp. of the chicken mixture just before serving.

Makes 2 doz. or 8 servings, 3 topped crackers each.

Substitute: Prepare as directed, substituting 2 small marinated sun-dried tomatoes, finely chopped, for the roasted red peppers.

Nutrition Information Per Serving: 90 calories, 2.5g total fat, 0g saturated fat, 105mg sodium, 12g carbohydrate, 5g protein.

RITZ CHEESY-CRAB TOPPER

Prep: 10 min. ● Total: 1 hour 10 min. (incl. refrigerating)

4 oz. (½ of 8 oz. pkg.) **PHILADELPHIA** Cream Cheese, softened

¼ cup **BREAKSTONE'S** or **KNUDSEN** Sour Cream

1 can (6 oz.) crabmeat, drained, flaked

¼ cup chopped fresh parsley

1 Tbsp. **KRAFT** 100% Grated Parmesan Cheese

3 drops hot pepper sauce

48 **RITZ** Crackers

MIX all ingredients except crackers; cover.

REFRIGERATE at least 1 hour.

SPOON about 1 tsp. of the crabmeat mixture onto each cracker just before serving.

Makes 4 doz. or 16 servings, 3 topped crackers each.

Substitute: Don't have canned crabmeat? Use 1 (6 oz.) can white tuna in water instead.

Nutrition Information Per Serving: 90 calories, 6g total fat, 2.5g saturated fat, 140mg sodium, 7g carbohydrate, 3g protein.

ROAST BEEF, ARUGULA AND BLUE CHEESE TOPPERS

Prep: 10 min. ● Total: 10 min.

12 **TRISCUIT** Rosemary & Olive Oil Crackers

12 baby arugula leaves

 3 thin slices deli roast beef (about 2½ oz.), quartered

 1 Tbsp. **KRAFT** Light **ROKA** Blue Cheese Reduced Fat Dressing

 3 grape or cherry tomatoes, quartered

TOP crackers with remaining ingredients.

SERVE immediately.

Makes 1 doz. or 4 servings, 3 topped crackers each.

Substitute: Prepare as directed, using thinly sliced leftover cooked roast beef or steak.

Nutrition Information Per Serving: 110 calories, 4g total fat, 1g saturated fat, 120mg sodium, 11g carbohydrate, 7g protein.

MANDARIN ALMOND-CHICKEN BITES

Prep: 10 min. ● Total: 1 hour 10 min. (incl. refrigerating)

½ cup finely chopped cooked chicken

½ cup drained canned mandarin orange segments, chopped

¼ cup dried cranberries

2 Tbsp. **PLANTERS** Sliced Almonds

2 Tbsp. **MIRACLE WHIP** Light Dressing

48 **TRISCUIT** Crackers

MIX chicken, oranges, cranberries, almonds and dressing; cover.

REFRIGERATE at least 1 hour.

TOP each cracker with 1 tsp. of the chicken mixture just before serving.

Makes 4 doz. or 16 servings, 3 topped crackers each.

Make Ahead: Chicken mixture can be stored in refrigerator up to 24 hours before spooning onto crackers as directed.

Nutrition Information Per Serving: 90 calories, 3.5g total fat, 0.5g saturated fat, 110mg sodium, 12g carbohydrate, 3g protein.

Jazz It Up:

Garnish topped crackers with a parsley sprig.

RITZ HOLIDAY BELL

Prep: 10 min. ● Total: 10 min.

- **6** slices **OSCAR MAYER** Hard Salami
- **1** pkg. (6 oz.) **KRAFT** Cracker Cuts Mild Cheddar Cheese
- **18** **RITZ** Crackers
- **18** thin red pepper strips
- **2** tsp. chopped fresh parsley

CUT 3 small bell-shaped pieces out of each salami slice and 1 small bell-shaped piece out of each cheese slice, using small cookie cutter or sharp knife.

TOP crackers with salami and cheese.

DECORATE with the peppers and parsley.

Makes 1½ doz. or 6 servings, 3 topped crackers each.

Fun Idea: Not sure what to do with the cheese after the cutouts are removed from the cheese slices? Fill them with additional salami bells and place on top of additional **RITZ** Crackers.

Nutrition Information Per Serving: 120 calories, 9g total fat, 4g saturated fat, 260mg sodium, 6g carbohydrate, 5g protein.

Jazz It Up:

Use a variety of small, holiday-shaped cookie cutters such as trees, ornaments and stars for a festive look.

TASTEFUL
TRADITIONS

**Classic desserts made better by adding
your favorite cookies "all dressed up"**

EASY CHOCOLATE ÉCLAIR SQUARES

Prep: 30 min. ● Total: 3 hours 30 min. (incl. refrigerating)

- 2 **cups cold milk, divided**
- 1 **pkg. (4-serving size) JELL-O Vanilla Flavor Instant Pudding & Pie Filling**
- 1 **tub (8 oz.) COOL WHIP Whipped Topping, thawed**
- 22 **HONEY MAID Honey Grahams**
- 4 **squares BAKER'S Unsweetened Chocolate**
- ¼ **cup (½ stick) butter or margarine**
- 1½ **cups powdered sugar**

POUR 1¾ cups of the milk into large bowl. Add dry pudding mix. Beat with wire whisk 2 min. Gently stir in whipped topping. Layer one-third of the grahams and half of the whipped topping mixture in 13×9-inch pan, breaking grahams as necessary to fit; repeat layers. Top with remaining grahams.

MICROWAVE chocolate and butter in medium microwaveable bowl on HIGH 1½ min., stirring after 1 min. Stir until chocolate is completely melted. Add sugar and remaining ¼ cup milk; stir until well blended. Immediately spread over grahams.

REFRIGERATE at least 4 hours or overnight. Store any leftover dessert in refrigerator.

Makes 24 servings, 1 square each.

Nutrition Information Per Serving: 180 calories, 8g total fat, 5g saturated fat, 170mg sodium, 27g carbohydrate, 2g protein.

Latte Éclair Squares:

Prepare as directed, substituting ¾ cup chilled, brewed, double-strength MAXWELL HOUSE Coffee for ¾ cup of the milk used to prepare the pudding.

RITZ ANGEL PIE

Prep: 15 min. ● Total: 45 min.

- **3** egg whites
- **½** tsp. vanilla
- **1** cup sugar
- **24** **RITZ** Crackers, finely crushed (about 1 cup)
- **1** cup finely chopped **PLANTERS** Pecans
- **¼** tsp. **CALUMET** Baking Powder
- **1½** cups thawed **COOL WHIP** Whipped Topping

PREHEAT oven to 350°F. Beat egg whites in large bowl with electric mixer on high speed until soft peaks form. Blend in vanilla. Gradually add sugar, beating after each addition until well blended. Continue to beat until stiff peaks form. Mix cracker crumbs, pecans and baking powder. Add to egg white mixture; stir gently until well blended. Spread into greased 9-inch pie plate.

BAKE 30 min. Cool completely.

TOP with the whipped topping just before serving. Store any leftover dessert in refrigerator.

Makes 8 servings, 1 slice each.

Nutrition Information Per Serving (with raspberry sauce): 310 calories, 16g total fat, 4g saturated fat, 125mg sodium, 41 g carbohydrate, 4g protein.

Jazz It Up:

Toss 1½ cups (about half of 12 oz. pkg.) frozen raspberries with 2 tsp. sugar in microwaveable bowl. Microwave on HIGH 30 sec.; stir until raspberries are thawed and sugar is dissolved. Place in blender; cover. Blend until smooth. Strain to remove seeds, if desired. Drizzle over pie just before serving. Garnish with a few fresh raspberries.

WHITE & BLACK-TIE-AFFAIR PIE

Prep: 30 min. ● Total: 5 hours (incl. refrigerating)

57 **NILLA** Wafers, divided

2 Tbsp. sugar

¼ cup (½ stick) butter or margarine, melted

2 cups cold milk, divided

1 pkg. (4-serving size) **JELL-O** White Chocolate Flavor Instant Pudding & Pie Filling

1 tub (8 oz.) **COOL WHIP** Whipped Topping, thawed, divided

1 pkg. (4-serving size) **JELL-O** Chocolate Flavor Instant Pudding & Pie Filling

2 squares **BAKER'S** Semi-Sweet Chocolate

CRUSH 35 of the wafers. Mix crumbs with sugar and butter until well blended. Press firmly onto bottom and up side of 9-inch pie plate. Pour 1 cup of the milk into medium bowl. Add dry white chocolate flavor pudding mix. Beat with wire whisk 2 min. or until well blended. (Mixture will be thick.) Add 1 cup of the whipped topping; stir gently until well blended. Spread evenly onto bottom of crust. Top with 12 of the remaining wafers.

POUR remaining 1 cup milk into separate medium bowl. Add remaining dry pudding mix. Beat with wire whisk 2 min. Gently stir in 1 cup of the remaining whipped topping; spread evenly over wafer layer. Refrigerate at least 3 hours. Meanwhile, melt chocolate as directed on package. Dip one-third of each of the remaining 10 wafers in chocolate. Turn wafers slightly, then dip the opposite side of each wafer in chocolate, leaving a V-shaped portion of each wafer uncoated in the center. Use a wooden toothpick to decorate wafers with some of the remaining chocolate to resemble bow ties. Add "buttons" with small drops of the remaining chocolate. Place on waxed paper-covered baking sheets; let stand until chocolate is firm.

TOP pie with remaining whipped topping just before serving. Garnish with decorated wafers. Store any leftover dessert in refrigerator.

Makes 10 servings, 1 slice each.

Nutrition Information Per Serving: 340 calories, 16g total fat, 10g saturated fat, 450mg sodium, 48g carbohydrate, 3g protein.

Jazz It Up:

Garnish with colored sprinkles just before serving.

HOLIDAY "EGGNOG" SQUARES

Prep: 15 min. ● Total: 3 hours 15 min. (incl. refrigerating)

- **67 NILLA** Wafers, divided
- ¼ cup (½ stick) butter or margarine, divided
- 2 Tbsp. sugar
- 3 squares **BAKER'S** White Chocolate
- 2 cups cold milk
- 2 pkg. (4-serving size each) **JELL-O** Vanilla Flavor Instant Pudding & Pie Filling
- ¾ tsp. rum extract
- ¼ tsp. ground nutmeg
- 1½ cups thawed **COOL WHIP** Whipped Topping

CRUSH 35 of the wafers; place in medium bowl. Melt 3 Tbsp. of the butter. Add to wafer crumbs along with the sugar; mix well. Spoon into 9-inch square pan; press firmly onto bottom of pan. Set aside.

PLACE chocolate and remaining 1 Tbsp. butter in small microwaveable bowl. Microwave on HIGH 1 min. or until butter is melted. Stir until chocolate is completely melted and mixture is well blended. Drizzle over crust.

POUR milk into large bowl. Add dry pudding mixes, extract and nutmeg. Beat with wire whisk 2 min. Gently stir in whipped topping. Spread half of the pudding mixture over chocolate layer; top with 16 of the remaining wafers. Cover with remaining pudding mixture. Refrigerate at least 3 hours or until firm. Cut into squares just before serving. Garnish with the remaining 16 wafers. Store any leftover dessert in refrigerator.

Makes 16 servings, 1 square each.

Nutrition Information Per Serving (without cookie dipped in chocolate): 210 calories, 9g total fat, 5g saturated fat, 280mg sodium, 31g carbohydrate, 2g protein.

Jazz It Up:

Prepare dessert and refrigerate as directed. Meanwhile, partially dip the remaining 16 wafers in additional melted BAKER'S White Chocolate. Immediately sprinkle coated portions of wafers with sprinkles. Let stand until chocolate is firm. Store at room temperature until ready to use as directed.

OREO CHOCOLATE CHEESECAKE

Prep: 30 min. ● Total: 6 hours 15 min. (incl. refrigerating)

38 OREO Chocolate Sandwich Cookies, divided

  5 Tbsp. butter or margarine, melted

  5 squares **BAKER'S** Semi-Sweet Chocolate, divided

  1 pkg. (8 oz.) **PHILADELPHIA** Cream Cheese, softened

 ½ cup sugar

1½ cups **BREAKSTONE'S** or **KNUDSEN** Sour Cream, divided

  2 eggs

  1 tsp. vanilla

  2 Tbsp. sugar

PREHEAT oven to 325°F, if using a silver 9-inch springform pan (or to 300°F if using a dark nonstick 9-inch springform pan). Finely crush 24 of the cookies; mix with butter. Press firmly onto bottom of pan. Stand remaining 14 cookies around inside edge of pan, firmly pressing bottom edge of each cookie into crust. Set aside.

MELT 4 of the chocolate squares in small saucepan on low heat; set aside. Beat cream cheese and ½ cup sugar in large bowl with electric mixer on medium speed until well blended. Add ½ cup of the sour cream, the eggs and vanilla; beat until well blended. Add melted chocolate; mix well. Pour over crust.

BAKE 35 to 40 min. or until top of cheesecake is slightly puffed and center is almost set. Mix remaining 1 cup sour cream and the 2 Tbsp. sugar; spread over cheesecake. Bake an additional 5 min. Run knife or metal spatula around rim of pan to loosen cake; cool before removing rim.

MELT remaining chocolate square; drizzle over cheesecake. Refrigerate at least 4 hours. Garnish with fresh raspberries, chocolate curls and fresh mint just before serving, if desired. Store any leftover dessert in refrigerator.

Makes 14 servings, 1 slice each.

Nutrition Information Per Serving (without garnish): 380 calories, 25g total fat, 12g saturated fat, 300mg sodium, 37g carbohydrate, 5g protein.

How to Make Chocolate Curls:

Let additional square(s) of BAKER'S Semi-Sweet Chocolate come to room temperature. Carefully draw a vegetable peeler at an angle across the chocolate square to make curls.

HOLIDAY BLACK FOREST PIE

Prep: 15 min. ● Total: 3 hours 15 min. (incl. refrigerating)

34 **OREO** Chocolate Sandwich Cookies, divided

¼ cup (½ stick) butter or margarine, melted

2 cups cold milk

2 pkg. (4-serving size each) or 1 pkg. (8-serving size) **JELL-O** Chocolate Flavor Instant Pudding & Pie Filling

1 tub (8 oz.) **COOL WHIP** Whipped Topping, thawed, divided

1 cup cherry pie filling

1 square **BAKER'S** Semi-Sweet Chocolate, melted

CUT 10 of the cookies into quarters; set aside for later use. Finely crush remaining 24 cookies; mix with the butter. Press firmly onto bottom and up side of 9-inch pie plate. Refrigerate while preparing filling.

POUR milk into large bowl. Add dry pudding mixes. Beat with wire whisk 2 min. or until well blended. (Mixture will be thick.) Spoon 1½ cups of the pudding into crust. Top with the reserved cookie pieces. Gently stir 1½ cups of the whipped topping into remaining pudding; spoon over pie.

REFRIGERATE 3 hours. Cover with remaining whipped topping just before serving. Top with the cherry pie filling. Drizzle with melted chocolate. Store any leftover dessert in refrigerator.

Makes 10 servings, 1 slice each.

Shortcut: Substitute 1 pkg. (6 oz.) **OREO** Pie Crust for the homemade crumb crust.

Nutrition Information Per Serving: 420 calories, 18g total fat, 11g saturated fat, 600mg sodium, 64g carbohydrate, 4g protein.

How to Make Mess-Free Cookie Crumbs:

Crushing cookies into crumbs can be a messy task. To keep the crumbs contained, place the whole cookies in a resealable plastic bag. Squeeze the air from the bag, and seal the bag. Run a rolling pin back and forth over the cookies until finely crushed.

LEMON-GINGER REFRIGERATOR ROLL

Prep: 20 min. ● Total: 8 hours 20 min. (incl. refrigerating)

1   cup cold fat-free milk

1   pkg. (4-serving size) JELL-O Lemon Flavor Instant Pudding & Pie Filling

1½ cups thawed COOL WHIP LITE Whipped Topping

30 NABISCO Ginger Snaps

POUR milk into medium bowl. Add dry pudding mix. Beat with wire whisk 2 min. or until well blended. Gently stir in whipped topping.

SPREAD about 1½ tsp. of the pudding mixture onto each cookie. Begin stacking cookies together, standing on edge on serving platter to make a log. Frost with remaining pudding mixture.

REFRIGERATE at least 8 hours or overnight. Cut diagonally into 12 slices to serve. Store any leftover dessert in refrigerator.

Makes 12 servings, 1 slice each.

Make Ahead: Be sure to refrigerate this dessert at least 8 hours before serving to allow the cookies to soften to the desired cake-like texture.

Nutrition Information Per Serving: 130 calories, 3g total fat, 1.5g saturated fat, 260mg sodium, 25g carbohydrate, 2g protein.

PHILADELPHIA WHITE CHOCOLATE-PEPPERMINT CHEESECAKE

Prep: 15 min. ● Total: 5 hours 35 min.

1½ cups **HONEY MAID** Graham Cracker Crumbs

3 Tbsp. sugar

¼ cup (½ stick) butter, melted

4 pkg. (8 oz. each) **PHILADELPHIA** Cream Cheese, softened

1 cup sugar

¼ tsp. peppermint extract

1 cup **BREAKSTONE'S** or **KNUDSEN** Sour Cream

4 squares **BAKER'S** White Chocolate, melted

4 eggs

1 cup thawed **COOL WHIP** Whipped Topping

16 starlight mints

HEAT oven to 325°F.

LINE 13×9-inch pan with foil, with ends of foil extending over sides of pan. Mix graham crumbs, 3 Tbsp. sugar and butter; press onto bottom of pan. Bake 10 min.

BEAT cream cheese, 1 cup sugar and extract in large bowl with mixer until well blended. Add sour cream and chocolate; mix well. Add eggs, 1 at a time, mixing on low speed after each just until blended. Pour over crust.

BAKE 40 min. or until center is almost set. Cool. Refrigerate 4 hours. Use foil handles to lift cheesecake from pan before cutting to serve. Top each piece with a dollop of **COOL WHIP** and a mint just before serving.

Makes 16 servings.

Serving Suggestion:

This is a great dessert to share at a holiday party. At 16 servings, there's enough for a crowd.

GIFT-GIVING
FAVORITES

**Great-tasting, innovative
gifts from your kitchen**

EASY OREO TRUFFLES

Prep: 30 min. ● Total: 1 hour 30 min. (incl. refrigerating)

1 pkg. (1 lb. 2 oz.) **OREO** Chocolate Sandwich Cookies, finely crushed, divided

1 pkg. (8 oz.) **PHILADELPHIA** Cream Cheese, softened

2 pkg. (8 squares each) **BAKER'S** Semi-Sweet Chocolate, melted

MIX 3 cups of the cookie crumbs and the cream cheese until well blended. Shape into 42 (1-inch) balls.

DIP balls in melted chocolate; place on waxed paper-covered baking sheet. (Any leftover melted chocolate can be stored in tightly covered container at room temperature and saved for another use.) Sprinkle with remaining cookie crumbs.

REFRIGERATE 1 hour or until firm. Store any leftover truffles in tightly covered container in refrigerator.

Makes 3½ doz. or 42 servings, 1 truffle each.

Nutrition Information Per Serving: 100 calories, 6g total fat, 3g saturated fat, 85mg sodium, 12g carbohydrate, 1g protein.

Jazz It Up:

Sprinkle truffles with colored sugar or sprinkles in addition to or in place of the cookie crumbs.

OREO CANDY CANE BARK

Prep: 10 min ● Total: 4 hours 10 min (incl. refrigerating)

3 pkg. (6 oz. each) **BAKER'S** White Chocolate

15 **OREO** Chocolate Sandwich Cookies, coarsely chopped (about 2 cups)

3 candy canes, crushed (about ¼ cup)

COVER large baking sheet with foil; set aside. Microwave chocolate in large microwaveable bowl on HIGH 2 min. or until almost melted, stirring every 30 sec. Stir until chocolate is completely melted. Stir in chopped cookies.

SPREAD immediately onto prepared baking sheet. Sprinkle with crushed candy canes; press candy lightly into chocolate with back of spoon.

REFRIGERATE 4 hours or until firm. Break into pieces. Store in tightly covered container in refrigerator.

Makes 1½ lb. or 18 servings.

Substitute: Prepare as directed, substituting 10 starlight mint candies for the candy canes.

Make Ahead: Bark can be stored in refrigerator up to 2 weeks.

Nutrition Information Per Serving: 210 calories, 11 g total fat, 6g saturated fat, 70mg sodium, 27g carbohydrate, 2g protein.

How to Easily Crush Candy Canes:

Crushing candy canes can be a messy task. To keep the crushed candy contained, place candy canes in a resealable plastic bag and squeeze air from bag; seal. Use a rolling pin or meat mallet to crush the candy into small pieces.

HONEY MAID "GINGERBREAD"

Prep: 10 min. ● Total: 1 hour 10 min. (incl. cooling)

18 **HONEY MAID** Gingerbread Grahams, finely crushed (about 2¼ cups)

¼ cup flour

¼ cup granulated sugar

2 tsp. **CALUMET** Baking Powder

¼ tsp. baking soda

1 cup fat-free milk

1 egg, lightly beaten

2 Tbsp. honey

2 to 3 tsp. water, divided

½ cup powdered sugar

PREHEAT oven to 350°F. Mix graham crumbs, flour, granulated sugar, baking powder and baking soda in medium bowl. Add milk, egg and honey; stir just until blended. Spoon into 3 lightly greased 5½×3¼×2-inch disposable mini loaf pans.

BAKE 30 min. or until wooden toothpick inserted into centers comes out clean. Cool completely.

ADD 2 tsp. of the water to powdered sugar; stir until well blended. Add remaining 1 tsp. water, if necessary, until glaze is of desired consistency. Drizzle over cooled loaves. Let stand until glaze is firm.

Makes 12 servings or 3 loaves, 4 servings each.

Nutrition Information Per Serving (with glaze): 170 calories, 2.5g total fat, 0.5g saturated fat, 280mg sodium, 34g carbohydrate, 3g protein.

Jazz It Up:

This "gingerbread" makes a great gift to bring to a holiday party. Cool completely and wrap in plastic wrap before placing in a holiday-themed basket or container.

LEMON-COCONUT SQUARES

Prep: 10 min. • Total: 3 hours 40 min. (incl. refrigerating)

35 NILLA Wafers, finely crushed (about 1⅓ cups)

1 cup sugar, divided

¼ cup (½ stick) butter or margarine, melted

1 tsp. grated lemon peel

2 eggs

¼ cup lemon juice

2 Tbsp. flour

½ tsp. **CALUMET** Baking Powder

¼ tsp. salt

⅓ cup **BAKER'S ANGEL FLAKE** Coconut

PREHEAT oven to 350°F. Mix wafer crumbs, ¼ cup of the sugar, the butter and lemon peel until well blended. Press firmly into 8-inch square baking pan. Bake 8 min.

BEAT eggs and remaining ¾ cup sugar in small bowl with wire whisk until thickened and well blended. Add lemon juice, flour, baking powder and salt; mix well. Pour over crust; sprinkle with coconut.

BAKE 25 to 30 min. or until center is set and top is lightly browned. Cool completely. Cover and refrigerate several hours or until chilled before cutting to serve. Store in tightly covered container in refrigerator.

Makes 20 servings, 1 square each.

Nutrition Information Per Serving: 110 calories, 4.5g total fat, 2g saturated fat, 95mg sodium, 16g carbohydrate, 1g protein.

PLANTERS DOUBLE FANTASY FUDGE

Prep: 30 min. ● Total: 4 hours 30 min. (incl. cooling)

- **6 cups sugar, divided**
- **1½ cups (3 sticks) butter or margarine, divided**
- **2 small cans (5 oz. each) evaporated milk (about ⅔ cup each)**
- **1 cup peanut butter**
- **2 jars (7 oz. each) JET-PUFFED Marshmallow Creme, divided**
- **2 cups chopped PLANTERS Dry Roasted Peanuts, divided**
- **2 tsp. vanilla, divided**
- **1½ pkg. (12 squares) BAKER'S Semi-Sweet Chocolate**

LINE 13×9-inch pan with foil, with ends of foil extending over sides of pan. Place 3 cups of the sugar, ¾ cup (1½ sticks) of the butter and 1 can of the evaporated milk in heavy 3-qt. saucepan. Bring to full rolling boil on medium heat, stirring constantly. Boil 4 min. or until candy thermometer reaches 234°F, stirring constantly to prevent scorching. Remove from heat.

ADD peanut butter and contents of 1 of the marshmallow creme jars; stir until completely melted. Add 1 cup of the peanuts and 1 tsp. of the vanilla; mix well. Pour immediately into prepared pan; spread to evenly cover bottom of pan. Set aside.

PLACE remaining 3 cups sugar, the remaining ¾ cup (1½ sticks) butter and the remaining can of evaporated milk in large heavy saucepan. Bring to full rolling boil on medium heat, stirring constantly. Boil 4 min. or until candy thermometer reaches 234°F, stirring constantly to prevent scorching. Remove from heat.

ADD chocolate and remaining jar of marshmallow creme; stir until completely melted. Add ½ cup of the remaining peanuts and the remaining 1 tsp. vanilla; mix well. Pour immediately over peanut butter fudge layer in pan. Spread to evenly cover peanut butter fudge; sprinkle with remaining ½ cup peanuts. Cool at room temperature at least 4 hours before cutting into small pieces to serve. Store in tightly covered container at room temperature.

Makes 6 lb. or 70 servings, 1 piece each.

Important Note: If you are only able to purchase a large (12 oz.) can of evaporated milk, be sure to use only ⅔ cup for each fudge layer so that the fudge will set.

High Altitude: For every 1,000 feet above sea level, decrease final recommended cooking temperature by 2°F.

Nutrition Information Per Serving: 190 calories, 10g total fat, 3.5g saturated fat, 70mg sodium, 26g carbohydrate, 3g protein.

Cooking Know-How:

If you don't have a candy thermometer, bring sugar mixture to full rolling boil on medium heat, then begin timing 4 min. while mixture continues to boil, stirring constantly.

OREO HOLIDAY TREATS

Prep: 30 min. ● Total: 30 min.

8 OREO Pure Milk Chocolate Covered Sandwich Cookies or
OREO White Fudge Covered Chocolate Sandwich Cookies

Suggested decorations: decorating icings, holiday sprinkles,
colored sugars

DRAW stars, trees, holiday ornaments or wreaths on tops of cookies
with icing. Decorate with sprinkles or colored sugars, if desired.

Makes 8 servings, 1 cookie each.

Gift-Giving:

These decorative cookies make a great gift. Remove outer wrapping and plastic tray
from original cookie box; line box with parchment paper. Place decorated cookies
in mini holiday paper cupcake liners before placing in box. Wrap with colorful plastic
wrap and festive ribbon, attaching a candy cane or small holiday ornament to top of
package with the ribbon.

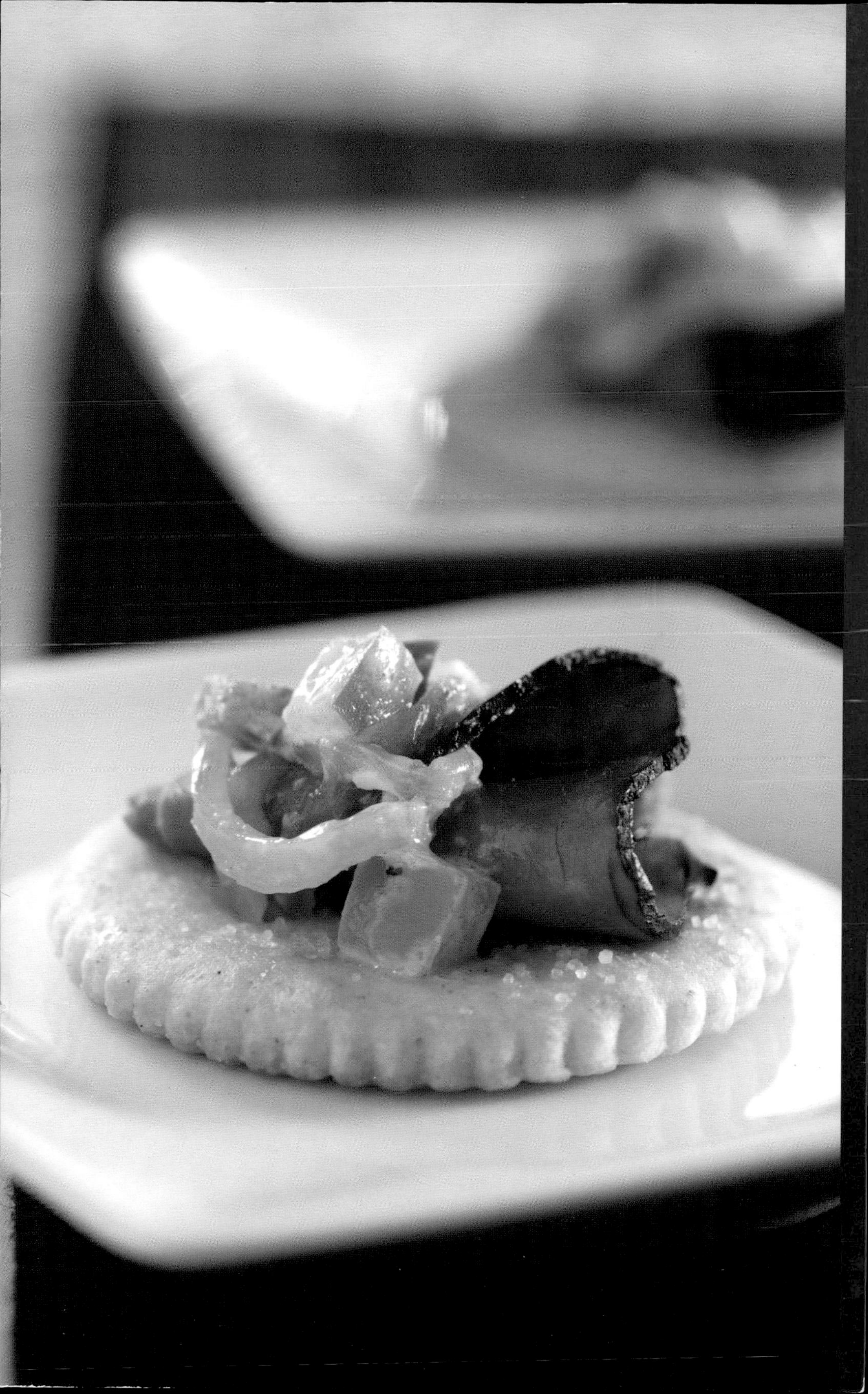

Small Bites & Party Food

Contents

94

'Tis the season for inviting family and friends over for a party. A successful gathering begins and ends with sensational food—and lets the hosts have fun, too. These savory appetizers and sweet treats make favorable first and last impressions while allowing you to enjoy every minute with your guests. Whether your entertaining style is formal or casual, or your event is small or large, you'll find the ideal recipes for your menu. Each chapter offers a selection of hot and cold appetizers along with delectable desserts and tips for make-ahead ease.

Hosting a cocktail party? Choose from an enticing array of finger foods that are easy to nibble while holding a drink. Sophisticated flavor pairings—such as caramelized onion and roast beef, and strawberries and chocolate—set the tone for a posh evening. Only you will know how simple everything was to prepare!

When the get-together is large and casual, serve a variety of crowd-pleasing toppers, dips, spreads, and sweets made with **NABISCO** Crackers and Cookies. Tantalize your guests' taste buds with ethnic inspirations from Mexico, Asia, Italy, and Greece, as well as all-American favorites with a flavor twist.

Set the stage perfectly for classic dinner parties with an offering of elegant starters that feature such sumptuous foods as shrimp, Brie cheese, and mushrooms. Then finish with a dazzling dessert that creates a lasting impression.

Finally, a gift from the kitchen—and the heart—is always appreciated. Package these sweet or savory treats decoratively to give guests as they leave your home. Or, bring them as hostess gifts to parties you attend.

As you gather with family and friends, cherish the time you spend together. And celebrate with these spectacular recipes for a party that sparkles with delicious memories.

Marianne Arimenta-Dente
Kraft Kitchens

Cocktail

Elegant bite-size nibbles—both sweet and savory—to enjoy while mingling

Sweet Dijon Cheddar & Pear Snacks

Prep: 5 min. **Total:** 5 min.

- 1 oz. **KRAFT** 2% Milk Cheddar Cheese, cut into 8 thin slices
- 8 **TRISCUIT** Crackers
- 8 thin pear slices
- 2 tsp. **GREY POUPON** Savory Honey Mustard

CUT cheese slices diagonally in half.

TOP crackers with cheese, pears and a dab of mustard.

Makes 4 servings, 2 topped crackers each.

Substitute: Substitute fruit chutney for the mustard.

How to Make Enough for a Crowd: This recipe is easily doubled or tripled to make enough for a party. Just increase all the ingredients proportionately.

NUTRITION INFORMATION PER SERVING: 70 calories, 3.5g total fat, 1g saturated fat, 120mg sodium, 9g carbohydrate, 3g protein.

Party

Caramelized Onion & Roast Beef Topper

Prep: 30 min. **Total:** 45 min. (incl. cooling)
---

 1 onion, thinly sliced

 2 Tbsp. each: chopped red and green bell peppers

 1 tsp. olive oil

 1 Tbsp. **BREAKSTONE'S** or **KNUDSEN** Sour Cream

 1 Tbsp. **GREY POUPON** Dijon Mustard

20 **RITZ** Crackers

 2 oz. thinly sliced deli roast beef, cut into 20 pieces

COOK vegetables in oil in nonstick skillet on medium-low heat 10 to 15 min. or until tender, stirring frequently. Cool.

STIR in sour cream and mustard.

COVER crackers with meat, folding as necessary to fit crackers. Top with vegetable mixture.

Makes 10 servings, 2 topped crackers each.

Make Ahead: Cooked vegetable mixture can be prepared ahead of time. Store in refrigerator up to 2 days before using as directed.

NUTRITION INFORMATION PER SERVING: 60 calories, 3g total fat, 0.5g saturated fat, 95mg sodium, 6g carbohydrate, 2g protein.

Special Extra: Garnish with chopped fresh parsley.

WHEAT THINS Salmon Snackers

Prep: 5 min. **Total:** 5 min.

6 **WHEAT THINS** Big Snack Crackers

2 Tbsp. **PHILADELPHIA** Light Cream Cheese Spread

1½ oz. smoked salmon, cut into 6 pieces

6 sprigs fresh dill

SPREAD crackers with cream cheese spread.

TOP with salmon and dill.

Makes 3 servings, 2 topped crackers each.

Substitute: Substitute chopped fresh chives for the dill.

How to Make Enough for a Crowd: This recipe is easily doubled or tripled to make enough for a party. Just increase all the ingredients proportionately.

NUTRITION INFORMATION PER SERVING: 60 calories, 3g total fat, 1g saturated fat, 210mg sodium, 5g carbohydrate, 4g protein.

Cocktail Party

Special Extra: Garnish with lemon zest or small strips of lemon peel.

California Shrimp Topper

Prep: 10 min. **Total:** 10 min.

   2 oz. (¼ of 8-oz. pkg.) **KRAFT** 2% Milk Sharp Cheddar Cheese, cut into 8 slices

 16 **TRISCUIT** Crackers

   8 thin avocado slices, cut in half

   8 cooked cleaned medium shrimp, cut lengthwise in half

   2 Tbsp. **TACO BELL® HOME ORIGINALS®** Thick 'N Chunky Salsa

CUT cheese slices diagonally in half.

TOP crackers with cheese, avocados, shrimp and salsa.

Makes 8 servings, 2 topped crackers each.

Substitute: Prepare using **TRISCUIT** Roasted Garlic Crackers.

NUTRITION INFORMATION PER SERVING: 80 calories, 4g total fat, 1.5g saturated fat, 150mg sodium, 8g carbohydrate, 4g protein.

TACO BELL® and HOME ORIGINALS® are trademarks owned and licensed by Taco Bell Corp.

Cocktail Party

Ham and Melon Toppers

Prep: 5 min. **Total:** 5 min.

- 2 slices cantaloupe (½ inch thick), each cut into thirds
- 3 slices **OSCAR MAYER** Shaved Brown Sugar Ham, cut in half
- 6 **WHEAT THINS** Big Snack Crackers
- 1½ tsp. **GREY POUPON** Honey Dijon Mustard

WRAP cantaloupe with ham; place on crackers.

TOP with mustard.

Makes 3 servings, 2 topped crackers each.

Substitute: Prepare using **SOCIABLES** Savory Crackers.

How to Make Enough for a Crowd: This recipe is easily doubled or tripled to make enough for a party. Just increase all the ingredients proportionately.

NUTRITION INFORMATION PER SERVING: 50 calories, 1.5g total fat, 0g saturated fat, 180mg sodium, 7g carbohydrate, 2g protein.

Cocktail Party

Fiesta Topper

Prep: 10 min. **Total:** 1 hour 10 min. (incl. refrigerating)

  4 oz. (½ of 8-oz. pkg.) **PHILADELPHIA** Neufchâtel Cheese, softened

  1 small carrot, shredded

 ½ cup shredded zucchini

 ⅓ cup finely chopped red bell peppers

  1 Tbsp. **KRAFT** Prepared Horseradish

45 **TRISCUIT** Crackers

MIX all ingredients except crackers.

REFRIGERATE 1 hour or until chilled.

SPREAD onto crackers.

Makes 15 servings, 3 topped crackers each.

Make it Easy: Look for pre-shredded or pre-cut vegetables on the salad bar in the produce section of your supermarket.

Substitute: Prepare using your favorite variety of **TRISCUIT** Thin Crisps.

NUTRITION INFORMATION PER SERVING: 80 calories, 4g total fat, 1.5g saturated fat, 135mg sodium, 11g carbohydrate, 2g protein.

Cocktail Party

Mini Broccoli & Ham Cups

Prep: 15 min. **Total:** 30 min.

 1 pkg. (10 oz.) frozen chopped broccoli, thawed, well drained

 ¼ cup chopped sun-dried tomatoes

 4 oz. (½ of 8-oz. pkg.) **PHILADELPHIA** Light Cream Cheese Spread

 1 Tbsp. **KRAFT** Grated Parmesan Cheese

 ¼ tsp. garlic powder

24 slices **OSCAR MAYER** Shaved Smoked Ham

 ⅓ cup chopped **PLANTERS** Smoked Almonds

HEAT oven to 350°F. Combine broccoli, tomatoes, cream cheese spread, Parmesan cheese and garlic powder.

FLATTEN ham slices. Press 1 ham slice onto bottom and up side of each of 24 miniature muffin pan cups. Fill with broccoli mixture; sprinkle with almonds.

BAKE 15 min. or until heated through.

Makes 2 doz. or 24 servings, 1 appetizer each.

Make Ahead: Having a party? Assemble appetizers several hours in advance; cover and refrigerate until ready to serve. Then, uncover and bake as directed.

NUTRITION INFORMATION PER SERVING: 30 calories, 2g total fat, 0.5g saturated fat, 160mg sodium, 2g carbohydrate, 3g protein.

Hot Crab Puffs

Prep: 5 min. **Total:** 7 min.

  2 green onions, sliced, divided

  ½ cup **KRAFT** 2% Milk Shredded Cheddar Cheese

  ½ cup **BREAKSTONE'S** or **KNUDSEN** Low Fat Cottage Cheese

  ½ cup **KRAFT** Light Mayo Reduced Fat Mayonnaise

  1 can (6 oz.) crabmeat, drained, flaked

  2 Tbsp. chopped roasted red peppers

  2 tsp. **KRAFT** Prepared Horseradish

 48 **TRISCUIT** Crackers

HEAT broiler. Reserve ½ the onions. Mix all remaining ingredients except crackers; spread onto crackers. Sprinkle with reserved onions.

BROIL, 4 inches from heat, 1 to 2 min. or until lightly browned.

Makes 4 doz. or 24 servings, 2 topped crackers each.

Use Your Microwave: Assemble as directed; place 8 topped crackers in single layer on microwaveable plate. Microwave each batch on HIGH 20 to 30 sec. or until crab mixture is heated through and cheese is melted.

Substitute: Prepare using **TRISCUIT** Cracked Pepper & Olive Oil Crackers.

NUTRITION INFORMATION PER SERVING: 70 calories, 3.5g total fat, 1g saturated fat, 150mg sodium, 7g carbohydrate, 3g protein.

Chai Latte Cups

Prep: 20 min. **Total:** 4 hours 20 min. (incl. refrigerating)

46 **NILLA** Wafers, divided

 2 Tbsp. **GENERAL FOODS INTERNATIONAL** Chai Latte

¼ cup hot water

 1 cup cold milk

 2 pkg. (3.4 oz. each) **JELL-O** White Chocolate Instant Pudding

 1 tub (8 oz.) **COOL WHIP** Whipped Topping, thawed

¼ tsp. ground cinnamon

ARRANGE 12 wafers on bottom of 9×5-inch loaf pan.

DISSOLVE latte mix in hot water in large bowl. Add milk and pudding mixes. Beat with whisk 2 min. Stir in the whipped topping. Spoon one-third of the pudding mixture over wafers in pan; top with 12 wafers. Repeat layers. Cover with remaining pudding.

REFRIGERATE at least 4 hours. Scoop ¼ cup pudding mixture into each of 10 (6-oz.) demitasse cups or cordial glasses. Add 1 wafer and a second scoop of pudding mixture to each cup. Sprinkle with cinnamon.

Makes 10 servings, ½ cup each.

Make it Easy: Use a small ice cream scoop to evenly portion the dessert into cups.

NUTRITION INFORMATION PER SERVING: 240 calories, 8g total fat, 6g saturated fat, 370mg sodium, 40g carbohydrate, 2g protein.

Sweet Endings

Special Extra: Garnish each with a cinnamon stick just before serving.

Double-Dipped Strawberries

Prep: 10 min. **Total:** 10 min.

10 fresh strawberries (about 1 pt.), washed, well dried

 4 squares **BAKER'S** Semi-Sweet Chocolate, melted

 8 **OREO** Cookies, coarsely crushed (about 1 cup crumbs)

DIP strawberries in melted chocolate; roll in crumbs.

PLACE on waxed paper-covered baking sheet; let stand until chocolate is firm.

Makes 10 servings, 1 dipped strawberry each.

Substitute: Prepare using **BAKER'S** White Chocolate.

Easy Microwave Melting of BAKER'S Chocolate Squares: Microwave 1 unwrapped square of **BAKER'S** Chocolate in microwaveable bowl on HIGH for 1 min., stirring after 30 sec. or until chocolate is almost melted. (The square will retain its shape.) Stir 1 min. or until chocolate is completely melted. Add 10 sec. for each additional square of chocolate, stirring every 30 sec.

NUTRITION INFORMATION PER SERVING: 110 calories, 5g total fat, 2.5g saturated fat, 55mg sodium, 14g carbohydrate, 1g protein.

Sweet Endings

Casual Celebrations

Quick and easy toppers, dips, spreads, and sweets sure to please any crowd

Fire-Roasted Avocado Toppers

Prep: 10 min. **Total:** 10 min.

- ¼ cup **KRAFT** Mayo with Olive Oil Reduced Fat Mayonnaise
- 1 avocado, chopped
- 4 cherry tomatoes, chopped
- 1 Tbsp. finely chopped cilantro
- 1 Tbsp. fresh lime juice
- 48 **TRISCUIT** Fire Roasted Tomato & Olive Oil Crackers

COMBINE all ingredients except crackers.

SPOON onto crackers.

Makes 24 servings, 2 topped crackers each.

NUTRITION INFORMATION PER SERVING: 60 calories, 3g total fat, 0g saturated fat, 65mg sodium, 8g carbohydrate, 1g protein.

Hot Layered Buffalo Spread

Prep: 10 min. **Total:** 12 min.

1 pkg. (8 oz.) **PHILADELPHIA** Cream Cheese, softened

1 cup chopped cooked chicken

1 Tbsp. hot pepper sauce

½ cup **ATHENOS** Crumbled Blue Cheese

2 Tbsp. chopped red bell peppers

   RITZ Crackers and celery sticks

SPREAD cream cheese onto microwaveable plate or bottom of 9-inch pie plate.

TOSS chicken with hot sauce; spoon over cream cheese. Top with blue cheese and bell peppers.

MICROWAVE on HIGH 1½ to 2 min. or until heated through. Serve with crackers and celery.

Makes about 2½ cups spread or 20 servings,
2 Tbsp. spread, 5 crackers and 5 celery sticks each.

Substitute: Substitute chopped **OSCAR MAYER** Southwestern Seasoned Chicken Breast Strips for the chopped cooked chicken.

NUTRITION INFORMATION PER SERVING: 150 calories, 9g total fat, 4g saturated fat, 250mg sodium, 11g carbohydrate, 5g protein.

Chinatown Chicken Wings

Prep: 15 min. **Total:** 40 min.

¾ cup **GOOD SEASONS** Asian Sesame with Ginger Dressing

¼ cup **KRAFT THICK 'N SPICY** Brown Sugar Barbecue Sauce

12 chicken wings (2 lb.), split, tips removed

½ cup **PLANTERS** Dry Roasted Peanuts, finely chopped

12 **RITZ** Crackers, crushed

HEAT oven to 400°F. Mix dressing and barbecue sauce in large bowl. Remove ½ cup dressing mixture. Add chicken to remaining dressing mixture; toss to coat.

MIX peanuts and cracker crumbs. Add wings, 1 at a time; turn until evenly coated. Place on baking sheet.

BAKE 20 to 25 min. or until cooked through. Serve with reserved dressing mixture.

Makes 12 servings, 2 wing pieces each.

Substitute: Substitute 1 lb. boneless, skinless chicken breasts, cut into 1-inch pieces, for the wing pieces. Bake 15 min. or until cooked through.

NUTRITION INFORMATION PER SERVING: 210 calories, 14g total fat, 3g saturated fat, 300mg sodium, 9g carbohydrate, 10g protein.

Baked Onion Dip

Prep: 20 min. **Total:** 45 min.

1 Tbsp. margarine

1 large sweet onion, finely chopped

⅓ cup **KRAFT** Light Mayo Reduced Fat Mayonnaise

½ cup **KRAFT** 2% Milk Shredded Cheddar Cheese

¼ cup **KRAFT** Grated Parmesan Cheese

1 Tbsp. chopped fresh parsley

½ tsp. hot pepper sauce

   TRISCUIT Thin Crisps

HEAT oven to 350°F. Melt margarine in large skillet on medium heat. Add onions; cook 5 to 7 min. or until golden brown, stirring occasionally. Cool slightly.

MIX mayo, cheeses, parsley and pepper sauce. Stir in onions. Spoon into baking dish.

BAKE 25 min. or until heated through. Serve with crackers.

Makes 1 cup dip or 8 servings, 2 Tbsp. dip and 15 crackers each.

Substitute: Prepare using **WHEAT THINS** Snack Crackers or **TRISCUIT** Thin Crisps Quattro Formaggio.

Make Ahead: Mix dip ingredients as directed; refrigerate up to 24 hours. When ready to serve, bake as directed increasing the baking time as needed until dip is heated through.

NUTRITION INFORMATION PER SERVING: 220 calories, 12g total fat, 3g saturated fat, 400mg sodium, 23g carbohydrate, 6g protein.

Four-Alarm RITZ Bites

Prep: 20 min. **Total:** 20 min.

¼ cup ketchup

1 chipotle pepper in adobo sauce, finely chopped

1 large clove garlic, minced

¼ cup **KRAFT** Real Mayo Mayonnaise

12 **RITZ** Crackers

1½ oz. **CRACKER BARREL** Sharp Cheddar Cheese, cut into 6 slices, halved diagonally

6 frozen cooked meatballs (½ oz. each), thawed, halved

MIX ketchup and peppers; set aside. Cook and stir garlic in small nonstick skillet on medium heat 1 to 2 min. or until golden brown. Remove from heat; stir in mayo.

PLACE crackers in single layer on microwaveable plate; top each with 1 cheese piece and meatball half, cut-side down. Microwave on HIGH 20 to 30 sec. or until cheese begins to melt.

TOP with ketchup and mayo mixtures.

Makes 6 servings, 2 topped crackers each.

Note: For milder flavor, use just ½ of a chipotle pepper.

How to Make Enough for a Crowd: This recipe is easily doubled or tripled to make enough for a party. Just increase all ingredients proportionately.

NUTRITION INFORMATION PER SERVING: 180 calories, 15g total fat, 4.5g saturated fat, 380mg sodium, 8g carbohydrate, 4g protein.

Casual Celebrations

Garden Ranch Dip

Prep: 10 min. **Total:** 3 hours 10 min. (incl. refrigerating)

- 1 container (16 oz.) **BREAKSTONE'S** Reduced Fat or **KNUDSEN** Light Sour Cream
- ½ cup finely chopped broccoli
- ¼ cup finely chopped carrots
- 2 green onions, finely chopped
- 2 Tbsp. finely chopped fresh parsley
- ¼ cup **KRAFT** Light Ranch Dressing
- **WHEAT THINS** Sundried Tomato & Basil Snack Crackers

MIX all ingredients except crackers. Refrigerate several hours or until chilled.

SERVE with crackers.

Makes 3 cups dip or 24 servings, 2 Tbsp. dip and 15 crackers each.

Substitute: Prepare using **WHEAT THINS** Ranch Snack Crackers, Multi-Grain Snack Crackers or Reduced Fat Baked Snack Crackers.

NUTRITION INFORMATION PER SERVING:
170 calories, 8g total fat, 2g saturated fat, 250mg sodium, 23g carbohydrate, 3g protein.

Last-Minute Cheesy Hot Dip

Prep: 10 min. **Total:** 25 min.

- 1 pkg. (8 oz.) **PHILADELPHIA** Cream Cheese, softened
- 1½ cups **KRAFT** Shredded Colby & Monterey Jack Cheese
- 5 green onions, thinly sliced
- ⅓ cup **KRAFT** Real Mayo Mayonnaise
- 1 Tbsp. **GREY POUPON** Harvest Coarse Ground Mustard
- 2 Tbsp. chopped **PLANTERS** Smoked Almonds
  RITZ Simply Socials Golden Wheat Crackers

HEAT oven to 350°F. Mix cheeses, onions, mayo and mustard in 9-inch pie plate; top with almonds.

BAKE 15 min. Serve with crackers.

Makes 2½ cups dip or 20 servings, 2 Tbsp. dip and 4 crackers each.

Serving Suggestion: Serve with **WHEAT THINS** Toasted Chips Multi-Grain.

NUTRITION INFORMATION PER SERVING: 170 calories, 12g total fat, 5g saturated fat, 290mg sodium, 11g carbohydrate, 4g protein.

Loaded "Baked Potato" Dip

Prep: 10 min. **Total:** 30 min.

½ cup instant potato flakes

½ cup milk

1 cup **BREAKSTONE'S** Reduced Fat or **KNUDSEN** Light Sour Cream

4 oz. (½ of 8-oz. pkg.) **PHILADELPHIA** Neufchâtel Cheese, softened

2 green onions, sliced, divided

1 cup **KRAFT** 2% Milk Shredded Sharp Cheddar Cheese

2 Tbsp. **OSCAR MAYER** Real Bacon Bits

   RITZ Toasted Chips Original

HEAT oven to 350°F. Mix potato flakes and milk in large bowl; let stand 5 min. or until milk is absorbed. Add sour cream, Neufchâtel cheese and half of the onions; mix well. (Dip will be soft set.)

SPOON into baking dish or 9-inch pie plate; sprinkle with shredded cheese and bacon bits.

BAKE 15 to 20 min. or until cheese is melted and dip is heated through. Sprinkle with remaining onions. Serve with the chips.

Makes 2¾ cups dip or 22 servings, 2 Tbsp. dip and 16 chips each.

Serving Suggestion: Serve with **WHEAT THINS** Snack Crackers.

Variation: Prepare as directed, substituting prepared mashed potatoes for the potato flakes and reducing the milk to 2 Tbsp.

NUTRITION INFORMATION PER SERVING: 180 calories, 8g total fat, 3g saturated fat, 390mg sodium, 23g carbohydrate, 4g protein.

Casual Celebrations

Greek Antipasto Dip

Prep: 10 min. **Total:** 22 min.

1 pkg. (8 oz.) **PHILADELPHIA** Neufchâtel Cheese, softened

1 clove garlic, finely chopped

⅓ cup chopped roasted red peppers

¼ cup finely chopped red onions

1 Tbsp. olive oil

¼ cup **ATHENOS** Crumbled Reduced Fat Feta Cheese

½ small lemon, seeded

1 Tbsp. minced fresh parsley

   WHEAT THINS Snack Crackers

HEAT oven to 350°F. Mix Neufchâtel cheese and garlic; spread onto bottom of 9-inch pie plate.

COVER with peppers and onions. Drizzle with oil; sprinkle with feta cheese.

BAKE 10 to 12 min. or until heated through. Squeeze lemon over dip. Sprinkle with parsley. Serve with crackers.

Makes 2 cups dip or 16 servings, 2 Tbsp. dip and 16 crackers each.

Serving Suggestion: Serve with **WHEAT THINS** Big Snack Crackers.

NUTRITION INFORMATION PER SERVING: 200 calories, 10g total fat, 3g saturated fat, 390mg sodium, 22g carbohydrate, 4g protein.

Casual Celebrations

Special Extra: Add a layer of 10 chopped kalamata or black olives to dip before baking as directed.

NILLA-Chocolate Tiramisu Cups

Prep: 30 min. **Total:** 4 hours 30 min. (incl. refrigerating)

- 4 squares **BAKER'S** Semi-Sweet Chocolate
- 1 Tbsp. butter or margarine
- 24 **NILLA** Wafers, divided
- 1 Tbsp. **MAXWELL HOUSE** Instant Coffee
- 2 Tbsp. hot water
- 1 pkg. (8 oz.) **PHILADELPHIA** Cream Cheese, softened
- ¼ cup sugar
- 1 tub (8 oz.) **COOL WHIP** Whipped Topping, thawed
- 6 fresh strawberries, halved

MICROWAVE chocolate and butter in microwaveable bowl on HIGH 1½ min., stirring after 1 min. Stir until chocolate is completely melted. Spoon into 12 foil cup-lined muffin cups; brush chocolate onto bottom and halfway up side of each cup. Place 1 wafer in each cup. Refrigerate until ready to use.

DISSOLVE coffee in hot water. Place cream cheese and sugar in medium bowl. Gradually add coffee, beating with whisk after each addition. Stir in whipped topping. Spoon ½ the cream cheese mixture into cups; top with remaining wafers and cream cheese mixture.

REFRIGERATE 4 hours or until set. Top with strawberries.

Makes 12 servings.

Make Ahead: Chocolate cups can be prepared ahead and stored, unfilled, in refrigerator up to 2 days.

NUTRITION INFORMATION PER SERVING (with NILLA Wafer garnish): 240 calories, 16g total fat, 10g saturated fat, 125mg sodium, 24g carbohydrate, 2g protein.

Sweet Endings

Special Extra: Top each cup with an additional NILLA Wafer just before serving.

OREO Cookie Cream Pie

Prep: 30 min. **Total:** 4 hours 30 min. (incl. refrigerating)

- 24 **OREO** Cookies, divided
- 2 Tbsp. butter or margarine, melted
- 2 cups cold milk
- 2 pkg. (3.4 oz. each) **JELL-O** White Chocolate Instant Pudding
- 2 cups thawed **COOL WHIP** Whipped Topping
- ½ cup fresh raspberries
- ½ square **BAKER'S** Semi-Sweet Chocolate, shaved into curls

CRUSH 16 cookies. Mix with butter; press onto bottom and up side of 9-inch pie plate. Chop 8 remaining cookies; set aside.

BEAT milk and pudding mixes with whisk 2 min. Stir in whipped topping and chopped cookies. Spoon into crust. Refrigerate 4 hours.

TOP with raspberries and chocolate curls just before serving.

Makes 10 servings.

How to Make Chocolate Curls: Warm a square of **BAKER'S** Baking Chocolate by microwaving it, unwrapped, on HIGH for a few seconds or just until you can smudge the chocolate with your thumb. Hold the square steadily and draw a peeler slowly over flat bottom of square, allowing a thin layer of chocolate to curl as it is peeled off the bottom of the square to make long, delicate curls. Use the same technique along the narrow side of the square to make short curls.

Substitute: Prepare using **BAKER'S** White Chocolate for the chocolate curls.

NUTRITION INFORMATION PER SERVING: 290 calories, 12g total fat, 7g saturated fat, 470mg sodium, 45g carbohydrate, 3g protein.

Sweet Endings

Mini Praline Cakes

Prep: 20 min. **Total:** 1 hour 8 min. (incl. cooling)

1½ cups **PLANTERS** Chopped Pecans

½ cup (1 stick) butter or margarine, melted

½ cup firmly packed brown sugar

1 pkg. (16 oz.) pound cake mix

½ cup water

½ cup **BREAKSTONE'S** or **KNUDSEN** Sour Cream

2 eggs

1½ cups caramel ice cream topping

1½ cups thawed **COOL WHIP** Whipped Topping

HEAT oven to 350°F. Combine pecans, butter and sugar; spoon into 24 well-greased and floured 2½-inch muffin cups. Beat cake mix, water, sour cream and eggs with mixer 3 min. Spoon into cups.

BAKE 15 to 18 min. or until toothpick inserted in centers comes out clean. Cool in pans on wire racks 15 min. Carefully loosen cakes and invert to remove from pans; cool completely.

DRIZZLE with caramel topping just before serving. Top with whipped topping.

Makes 2 doz. or 24 servings, 1 cake each.

Make Ahead: Cakes can be stored in refrigerator up to 3 days before topping as directed and serving.

NUTRITION INFORMATION PER SERVING: 260 calories, 13g total fat, 5g saturated fat, 150mg sodium, 34g carbohydrate, 3g protein.

Sweet Endings

Classic Entertaining

Sophisticated appetizers and desserts for extra-special celebrations

Asian Chicken Topper

Prep: 15 min. **Total:** 15 min.

- 30 Honey Butter **RITZ** Crackers
- 1 cucumber, cut into 30 thin slices, halved
- 6 oz. cooked chicken, thinly sliced, cut into 1½×1-inch pieces
- 2 Tbsp. **GOOD SEASONS** Asian Sesame with Ginger Dressing
- 1 green onion, sliced
- 1 Tbsp. finely chopped **PLANTERS** Honey Roasted Dry Roasted Peanuts

TOP crackers with cucumbers and chicken.

DRIZZLE with dressing.

SPRINKLE with onions and peanuts.

Makes 10 servings, 3 topped crackers each.

Creative Leftovers: This is a great way to use leftover cooked chicken.

NUTRITION INFORMATION PER SERVING: 100 calories, 5g total fat, 1g saturated fat, 90mg sodium, 8g carbohydrate, 6g protein.

Raspberry-Brie RITZ Toppers

Prep: 15 min. **Total:** 17 min.

24 **RITZ** Crackers or **RITZ** Snowflake Crackers

4 slices **OSCAR MAYER** Honey Ham, cut into 6 strips each

4 oz. Brie cheese, cut into 24 small pieces

2 Tbsp. raspberry preserves

2 Tbsp. **PLANTERS** Pistachio Lovers Mix, chopped

HEAT broiler. Top crackers with ham, folding as needed to fit crackers; cover with cheese. Place on baking sheet.

BROIL, 4 inches from heat, 1 to 1½ min. or until cheese begins to melt.

TOP with preserves and nuts.

Makes 2 doz. or 12 servings, 2 topped crackers each.

Easy No-Broil Preparation: These fruity Brie toppers are equally delicious without broiling. Assemble as directed, then serve at room temperature.

NUTRITION INFORMATION PER SERVING: 90 calories, 5g total fat, 2g saturated fat, 200mg sodium, 7g carbohydrate, 4g protein.

Special Extra: For variety, substitute fig jam for the raspberry preserves.

Garlic-Shrimp Cups

Prep: 35 min. **Total:** 1 hour 10 min.

---

   2 **eggs**
 ½ **cup water**
 24 **TRISCUIT Roasted Garlic Crackers**
   2 **oz. (¼ of 8-oz. pkg.) PHILADELPHIA Neufchâtel Cheese, softened**
 ¼ **tsp. lemon zest**
   2 **tsp. lemon juice**
   2 **tsp. fat-free milk**
   2 **tsp. chopped fresh parsley**
 24 **uncooked medium shrimp (about ½ lb.), peeled, deveined**
   2 **cloves garlic, minced**

HEAT oven to 350°F. Beat eggs and water in pie plate with whisk until blended. Add 12 crackers; let stand 8 min., turning over after 4 min. Press 1 soaked cracker onto bottom and up side of each of 12 mini muffin pan cups sprayed with cooking spray. Repeat with remaining 12 crackers in additional muffin cups.

BAKE 8 to 10 min. or until lightly browned. Use metal spatula to carefully loosen crusts from muffin pan; transfer to lightly greased baking sheet. Bake an additional 20 to 25 min. or until crisp. Remove to wire racks; cool.

MEANWHILE, mix Neufchâtel cheese, lemon zest, lemon juice, milk and parsley; set aside. Cook and stir shrimp and garlic in nonstick skillet sprayed with cooking spray on medium-high heat 3 to 4 min. or until shrimp turn pink. Place 1 shrimp in each cracker cup; top with Neufchâtel cheese mixture.

Makes 2 doz. or 24 servings, 1 shrimp cup each.

Make Ahead: Cooled baked cracker cups can be stored in airtight container at room temperature up to 8 hours. Cooked shrimp and Neufchâtel cheese mixture can be stored in separate containers in refrigerator until ready to use. When ready to serve, place 1 shrimp in each cup; place on baking

Classic Entertaining

sheet. Bake at 350°F for 7 to 8 min. or until shrimp are heated through before topping with Neufchâtel mixture.

Shortcut: In a hurry? Try this quick-and-easy variation instead. Omit eggs and water. Prepare Neufchâtel cheese mixture and cook shrimp as directed. Spread Neufchâtel cheese mixture onto crackers, then top with shrimp and sprinkle with parsley.

NUTRITION INFORMATION PER SERVING: 40 calories, 1.5g total fat, 0.5g saturated fat, 55mg sodium, 4g carbohydrate, 2g protein.

Warm Italian Vegetable & Cheese Dip

Prep: 15 min. **Total:** 30 min.

1 **small eggplant, chopped**

1 **cup chopped onions**

1 **cup chopped red bell peppers**

2 **cloves garlic, minced**

¼ **cup KRAFT Sun-Dried Tomato Dressing**

1 **zucchini, chopped**

1 **large tomato, chopped**

¼ **cup KRAFT Grated Parmesan Cheese**

½ **cup KRAFT Shredded Low-Moisture Part-Skim Mozzarella Cheese**

WHEAT THINS Big Snack Crackers

COOK and stir eggplant, onions, bell peppers and garlic in dressing in large skillet on medium heat 8 min.

STIR in zucchini and tomatoes; cover. Simmer 5 to 7 min. or until tender. Stir in Parmesan cheese.

SPOON into serving bowl. Sprinkle with mozzarella cheese. Serve with the crackers.

Makes 5 cups dip or 40 servings, 2 Tbsp. dip and 11 crackers each.

Serving Suggestion: Serve with **WHEAT THINS** Toasted Chips Multi-Grain.

Edible Dipper Bowl: Use a large red, green or yellow bell pepper as a unique serving bowl for dip. Remove top and seeds. Fill with dip just before serving.

NUTRITION INFORMATION PER SERVING: 160 calories, 7g total fat, 1.5g saturated fat, 310mg sodium, 23g carbohydrate, 3g protein.

Classic Entertaining

Stuffed Mushroom Dip

Prep: 15 min. **Total:** 20 min.

TRISCUIT Thin Crisps Parmesan Garlic

1 **Tbsp. butter**

1 **lb. mushrooms, finely chopped**

1 **red bell pepper, finely chopped**

1 **clove garlic, minced**

2 **Tbsp. KRAFT Grated Parmesan Cheese**

2 **Tbsp. BREAKSTONE'S Reduced Fat or KNUDSEN Light Sour Cream**

PLACE 30 crackers in resealable plastic bag. Use rolling pin to crush crackers; set aside.

MELT butter in large nonstick skillet on medium-high heat. Add mushrooms, bell peppers and garlic; cook 8 min. or until peppers are tender and liquid is evaporated, stirring occasionally. Remove from heat.

STIR in cracker crumbs, cheese and sour cream. Spoon into serving dish. Serve warm with additional crackers.

Makes 2 cups dip or 16 servings, 2 Tbsp. dip and 15 crackers each.

Make Ahead: Prepare dip as directed. Transfer to microwaveable dish; cool. Store, tightly covered, in refrigerator up to 24 hours. When ready to serve, uncover and microwave on HIGH 2 min. or until heated through.

NUTRITION INFORMATION PER SERVING: 170 calories, 7g total fat, 2g saturated fat, 220mg sodium, 26g carbohydrate, 5g protein.

Classic Entertaining

Holiday Fiesta Spread

Prep: 30 min. **Total:** 1 hour 30 min. (incl. refrigerating)

- 2 pkg. (8 oz. each) **PHILADELPHIA** Cream Cheese, softened
- 1 pkg. (1¼ oz.) **TACO BELL® HOME ORIGINALS®** Taco Seasoning Mix
- 1 cup **KRAFT** Mexican Style Shredded Cheese, divided
- ¾ cup **BREAKSTONE'S** or **KNUDSEN** Sour Cream
- ½ cup chopped avocados
- 2 Tbsp. sliced black olives
- 1 Tbsp. chopped red bell peppers
- 2 **WHEAT THINS** Snack Crackers

  RITZ Snowflake Crackers or **RITZ** Crackers

MIX cream cheese, seasoning mix and ½ cup shredded cheese; spread into Christmas tree shape on 10-inch plate. Top with sour cream to within ¼ inch of edges. Sprinkle with remaining shredded cheese around edges. Refrigerate at least 1 hour.

REMOVE from refrigerator about 15 min. before serving. Top with avocados, olives and bell peppers. Place **WHEAT THINS** at bottom of tree for the trunk.

SERVE with the remaining crackers.

Makes 3½ cups spread or 28 servings,
2 Tbsp. spread and 5 crackers each.

NUTRITION INFORMATION PER SERVING: 170 calories, 12g total fat, 6g saturated fat, 310mg sodium, 12g carbohydrate, 3g protein.

TACO BELL® and HOME ORIGINALS® are trademarks owned and licensed by Taco Bell Corp.

Classic Entertaining

Special Extra: Top this festive tree-shaped holiday spread with a red bell pepper star. Just cut a piece of red bell pepper into a star shape using a 1½-inch star-shaped cookie cutter. Or, cut the star from a KRAFT Singles.

Chicken Divan Toppers

Prep: 5 min. **Total:** 15 min.

- **2** oz. (⅓ of 6-oz. pkg.) **KRAFT** Natural 2% Milk Monterey Jack, Mild Cheddar & Colby Cheeses, cut into 8 slices

- **1** cooked small boneless, skinless chicken breast half (¼ lb.), cut into 16 slices

- **2** Tbsp. **BREAKSTONE'S** Reduced Fat or **KNUDSEN** Light Sour Cream

- **1** tsp. **GREY POUPON** Harvest Coarse Ground Mustard

- **16** **TRISCUIT** Rosemary & Olive Oil Crackers

- **16** small broccoli florets, cooked

HEAT oven to 350°F. Cut cheese slices diagonally in half. Toss chicken with sour cream and mustard.

PLACE crackers on baking sheet. Top with chicken, cheese and broccoli.

BAKE 8 to 10 min. or until cheese is melted.

Makes 8 servings, 2 topped crackers each.

Substitute: Substitute **KRAFT** Mayo with Olive Oil Reduced Fat Mayonnaise for the sour cream.

NUTRITION INFORMATION PER SERVING: 90 calories, 4g total fat, 1.5g saturated fat, 135mg sodium, 8g carbohydrate, 8g protein.

Special Extra: Sprinkle lightly with cracked black pepper or paprika before baking.

Marinated Antipasto Appetizers

Prep: 10 min. **Total:** 40 min. (incl. marinating)

- 4 oz. (½ of 8 oz. pkg.) **KRAFT** Low-Moisture Part-Skim Mozzarella Cheese, cut into 16 cubes
- 4 canned artichoke hearts, drained, quartered
- ¼ cup **KRAFT GOOD SEASONS** Italian Vinaigrette Dressing made with Extra Virgin Olive Oil
- 16 grape tomatoes
- 16 slices **OSCAR MAYER** Pepperoni

  RITZ Snowflake Crackers

COMBINE cheese, artichokes and dressing. Refrigerate 30 min. to marinate.

DRAIN cheese and artichokes; discard marinade. Thread 1 each tomato, artichoke quarter, pepperoni slice and cheese cube onto each of 16 small wooden skewers.

ARRANGE on platter. Serve with crackers.

Makes 16 servings, 1 skewer and 5 crackers each.

Substitute: Prepare using **RITZ** Simply Socials Original Crackers.

NUTRITION INFORMATION PER SERVING: 120 calories, 7g total fat, 2g saturated fat, 290mg sodium, 11g carbohydrate, 3g protein.

Classic Entertaining

Special Extra: If fresh rosemary sprigs are available, substitute them for the wooden skewers. Wash and dry 16 (4- to 6-inch-long) rosemary sprigs. Remove leaves, leaving just a few leaves at the end of each sprig. (Reserve rosemary leaves for another use.) Thread ingredients on sprigs as directed.

Chicken Parmesan Snackers

Prep: 10 min. **Total:** 16 min.

- 2 oz. (¼ of 8-oz. pkg.) **KRAFT** Mozzarella Cheese, cut into 8 slices
- 1 cooked small boneless, skinless chicken breast half (¼ lb.), cut into 16 thin slices
- ¼ cup spaghetti sauce
- 16 **TRISCUIT** Cracked Pepper & Olive Oil Crackers
- ½ tsp. dried oregano leaves

HEAT oven to 350°F. Cut cheese slices in half. Toss chicken with sauce.

PLACE crackers on baking sheet. Top with chicken, cheese and oregano.

BAKE 5 to 6 min. or until cheese is melted.

Makes 8 servings, 2 topped crackers each.

Use Your Microwave: Top crackers as directed. Place 8 crackers on microwaveable plate. Microwave on HIGH 10 to 15 sec. or until cheese is melted. Repeat with remaining topped crackers.

Substitute: Prepare using **TRISCUIT** Rosemary & Olive Oil Crackers or **RITZ** Crackers.

NUTRITION INFORMATION PER SERVING: 80 calories, 3.5g total fat, 1g saturated fat, 140mg sodium, 7g carbohydrate, 6g protein.

Chicken Sate Appetizers

Prep: 30 min. **Total:** 1 hour 10 min. (incl. marinating)

- 1 **cup chicken broth, divided**
- ½ **cup chopped onions**
- ¼ **cup soy sauce**
- 1 **clove garlic, minced**
- 4½ **tsp. minced peeled ginger**
- ½ **tsp. ground cumin**
- ½ **tsp. turmeric**
- 1 **lb. boneless, skinless chicken breasts, cut into 16 strips**
- ¼ **cup PLANTERS Dry Roasted Peanuts, chopped**
- 2 **Tbsp. light brown sugar**
- 2 **tsp. cornstarch**

MIX ½ cup broth, onions, soy sauce, garlic, ginger, cumin and turmeric. Place chicken in resealable plastic bag. Add half of the broth mixture; seal bag. Turn to evenly coat chicken. Refrigerate at least 30 min.

HEAT broiler. Remove chicken from marinade. Discard bag and marinade. Thread chicken onto 16 skewers. Place on rack of broiler pan.

BROIL 8 to 10 min. or until chicken is cooked through, turning occasionally. Meanwhile, mix remaining broth mixture, remaining broth, peanuts, sugar and cornstarch in saucepan; cook on medium-high heat until mixture comes to a boil and thickens, stirring occasionally. Serve with chicken.

Makes 16 servings, 1 skewer each.

How to Easily Cut Chicken: Cutting boneless, skinless chicken breasts into pieces can be a slippery task. Make it safer and prevent the knife from slipping by cutting the chicken while it is partially frozen. The firmer chicken is much easier to cut and handle.

NUTRITION INFORMATION PER SERVING: 60 calories, 2g total fat, 0g saturated fat, 240mg sodium, 3g carbohydrate, 7g protein.

Classic Entertaining

OREO Cheesecake Bites

Prep: 20 min. **Total:** 5 hours 5 min. (incl. refrigerating)

- 36 **OREO** Cookies, divided
- ½ cup (1 stick) butter or margarine, divided
- 4 pkg. (8 oz. each) **PHILADELPHIA** Cream Cheese, softened
- 1 cup sugar
- 1 tsp. vanilla
- 1 cup **BREAKSTONE'S** or **KNUDSEN** Sour Cream
- 4 eggs
- 4 squares **BAKER'S** Semi-Sweet Chocolate

HEAT oven to 325°F. Line 13×9-inch baking pan with foil. Finely crush 24 cookies. Melt ¼ cup butter; mix with crumbs. Press onto bottom of pan.

BEAT cream cheese, sugar and vanilla with mixer until blended. Add sour cream; mix well. Add eggs, 1 at a time, beating just until blended after each addition. Chop remaining cookies. Gently stir into batter; pour over crust.

BAKE 45 min. or until center is almost set. Cool. Meanwhile, place chocolate and remaining ¼ cup butter in microwaveable bowl. Microwave on HIGH 1 min. Stir until smooth. Cool slightly; pour over cheesecake. Spread to cover top of cheesecake. Refrigerate at least 4 hours. Remove cheesecake from pan before cutting to serve.

Makes 36 servings, 1 bar each.

How to Make Mess-Free Cookie Crumbs: Crushing cookies into crumbs can be a messy task. To keep the mess to a minimum, place the whole cookies in a resealable plastic bag. Flatten bag to remove excess air, then seal bag. Crush the cookies into crumbs by rolling a rolling pin across the bag until the crumbs are as fine as you need.

How to Neatly Cut Dessert Bars: When cutting creamy-textured bars, such as these cheesecake bites, carefully wipe off the knife blade between cuts with a clean damp towel. This prevents the creamy filling from building up on the blade, ensuring clean cuts that leave the edges intact.

Sweet Endings

Note: When lining pan with foil, extend ends of foil over sides of pan to use as handles when removing cheesecake from pan.

NUTRITION INFORMATION PER SERVING: 220 calories, 16g total fat, 9g saturated fat, 180mg sodium, 17g carbohydrate, 3g protein.

Brown Sugar Cheesecake Bars

Prep: 15 min. **Total:** 3 hours 46 min. (incl. refrigerating)

- 7 **HONEY MAID** Honey Grahams, crushed
- ⅔ cup granulated sugar, divided
- 3 Tbsp. butter, melted
- 2 pkg. (8 oz. each) **PHILADELPHIA** Cream Cheese, softened
- 1 tsp. vanilla
- 2 whole eggs
- 1 egg yolk
- ½ cup firmly packed brown sugar
- 1 Tbsp. water

HEAT oven to 350°F. Mix graham crumbs, 2 Tbsp. granulated sugar and butter. Press onto bottom of 9-inch square baking pan. Beat cream cheese, remaining granulated sugar and vanilla with mixer until blended. Add whole eggs and egg yolk; mix well. Pour over crust.

BAKE 30 min. or until center is almost set. Cool completely. Refrigerate at least 3 hours.

HEAT broiler. Mix brown sugar and water; spread over cheesecake. Broil, 6 inches from heat, 1 min. or until topping is hot and bubbly. Serve warm.

Makes 18 servings, 1 bar each.

Substitute: Prepare using **HONEY MAID** Cinnamon Grahams or 1 cup **HONEY MAID** Graham Cracker Crumbs.

NUTRITION INFORMATION PER SERVING: 190 calories, 12g total fat, 7g saturated fat, 150mg sodium, 19g carbohydrate, 3g protein.

Sweet Endings

CHIPS AHOY!
Warm S'Mores

Prep: 5 min. **Total:** 6 min.

16 **CHIPS AHOY! Cookies, divided**

 2 squares **BAKER'S Semi-Sweet Chocolate, chopped**

 2 tsp. **BAKER'S ANGEL FLAKE Coconut**

16 **JET-PUFFED Miniature Marshmallows**

PLACE 8 cookies, flat-sides up, on microwaveable plate; top with remaining ingredients.

MICROWAVE on HIGH 30 sec. or until chocolate is almost melted. Cover with remaining cookies; press down lightly to secure. Microwave 30 sec. or until cookies are warmed and chocolate and marshmallows are melted.

SERVE warm. Or, cover and refrigerate 5 to 10 min. or until filling is set.

Makes 8 servings.

Make it a Party: Place all ingredients in separate small bowls. If desired, add other filling choices, such as small candies and/or crushed **OREO** Cookies. Let the kids mix and match the filling ingredients as desired to create their own stuffed cookies!

Use Your Oven: Heat oven to 350°F. Top 8 cookies as directed; place on foil-covered baking sheet. Bake 4 min. Cover with remaining cookies; press down lightly to secure. Bake 2 to 4 min. or until cookies are warmed and chocolate and marshmallows are melted.

NUTRITION INFORMATION PER SERVING: 160 calories, 8g total fat, 3.5g saturated fat, 85mg sodium, 23g carbohydrate, 2g protein.

Sweet Endings

Gift-Giving

Sweet and savory treats from your kitchen to give as festive gifts

Chili Snack Mix

Prep: 10 min. **Total:** 20 min.

- 3 cups **PREMIUM** Mini Saltine Crackers
- 1 can (11.5 oz.) **PLANTERS** Mixed Nuts
- 3 Tbsp. butter, melted
- 1 tsp. chili powder
- ½ tsp. ground cumin
- ¼ tsp. garlic powder

HEAT oven to 375°F. Combine crackers and nuts in large bowl. Mix butter and seasonings. Drizzle over cracker mixture; toss to coat.

SPREAD into foil-lined 15×10×1-inch baking pan.

BAKE 10 min. or until lightly toasted, stirring after 5 min. Cool.

Makes 5 cups or 20 servings, ¼ cup each.

Gift-Giving Tip: Save cookie tins of all shapes and sizes throughout the year. Or, buy inexpensive jars, baking pans, mugs or festive serving dishes or bowls for packaging your edible gifts. The packaging then becomes a gift, too!

NUTRITION INFORMATION PER SERVING: 150 calories, 11g total fat, 2.5g saturated fat, 190mg sodium, 10g carbohydrate, 4g protein.

Special Extra: For a burst of flavor, add ¼ tsp. ground red pepper (cayenne) to cracker mixture along with the other seasonings.

OREO S'Mores Brownies

Prep: 15 min. **Total:** 45 min.

7½ **HONEY MAID** Honey Grahams, broken in half

1 pkg. (21 oz.) brownie mix

4 squares **BAKER'S** White Chocolate, chopped

1 cup **JET-PUFFED** Miniature Marshmallows

8 **OREO** Cookies, chopped, divided

HEAT oven to 350°F. Line 13×9-inch baking pan with foil; spray with cooking spray. Arrange graham squares in single layer in bottom of pan, overlapping slightly if necessary. Set aside.

PREPARE brownie batter as directed on package; stir in chopped chocolate, marshmallows and ¾ cup chopped cookies. Spread onto bottom of pan. Sprinkle with remaining cookies.

BAKE 27 to 30 min. or until toothpick inserted 1 inch from edge of pan comes out clean. Cool completely.

Makes 2 doz. or 24 servings, 1 brownie each.

Substitute: For more chocolate flavor, prepare with **BAKER'S** Semi-Sweet Chocolate.

NUTRITION INFORMATION PER SERVING: 220 calories, 10g total fat, 2.5g saturated fat, 125mg sodium, 32g carbohydrate, 2g protein.

RITZ Coconut Crackle

Prep: 15 min. **Total:** 55 min. (incl. cooling)

---

35 **RITZ** Crackers

½ **cup (1 stick) butter or margarine**

¾ **cup firmly packed light brown sugar**

1 **cup BAKER'S Semi-Sweet Chocolate Chunks**

¾ **cup BAKER'S ANGEL FLAKE Coconut, toasted**

HEAT oven to 350°F. Arrange crackers in greased 15×10×1-inch baking pan. Bring butter and sugar to boil in medium saucepan on medium heat; cook 2 min. Pour over crackers in prepared pan; spread to completely cover crackers. (Be careful—sugar mixture is very hot!)

BAKE 6 to 8 min. or until sugar mixture is lightly browned and bubbly. Sprinkle with chocolate; bake an additional 1 to 2 min. or until chocolate begins to melt. Remove from oven. Immediately spread chocolate over crackers.

SPRINKLE with coconut; press lightly into chocolate with back of spoon. Cool completely. Break into pieces. Store in tightly covered container at room temperature.

Makes 1¼ lb. or 14 servings.

How to Toast Coconut: Toasting coconut is easy. Just spread **BAKER'S ANGEL FLAKE** Coconut evenly in shallow baking pan. Bake at 350°F for 7 to 10 min. or until lightly browned, stirring frequently. Or, spread in microwaveable pie plate. Microwave on HIGH 3 min. or until lightly browned, stirring every minute. Watch carefully as coconut can easily burn!

Gift-Giving Tip: This easy-to-make treat makes a great gift for that special friend or teacher. Just pack in an airtight decorative container and wrap with colorful ribbon. Be sure to include a copy of the recipe since the recipient is sure to ask for it!

NUTRITION INFORMATION PER SERVING: 210 calories, 13g total fat, 8g saturated fat, 135mg sodium, 25g carbohydrate, 1g protein.

Gift-Giving

Peanut Butter Cookie Bars

Prep: 10 min. **Total:** 40 min.

½ **cup (1 stick) butter**

24 **NUTTER BUTTER** Peanut Butter Sandwich Cookies, divided

1½ cups **BAKER'S ANGEL FLAKE** Coconut

1 can (14 oz.) sweetened condensed milk

1 cup **BAKER'S** Semi-Sweet Chocolate Chunks

HEAT oven to 350°F. Melt butter in oven in foil-lined 13×9-inch baking pan.

CRUSH 12 cookies; sprinkle over butter. Top with coconut and milk. Coarsely chop remaining cookies; sprinkle over milk. Top with chocolate.

BAKE 25 to 30 min. or until lightly browned. Cool completely before cutting into bars.

Makes 32 servings, 1 bar each.

NUTRITION INFORMATION PER SERVING: 180 calories, 10g total fat, 6g saturated fat, 90mg sodium, 21g carbohydrate, 2g protein.

Gift-Giving

Herb-and-Nut Cream Cheese Log

Prep: 10 min. **Total:** 10 min.

- **1** pkg. (8 oz.) **PHILADELPHIA** Cream Cheese, softened
- ⅓ cup **KRAFT** Grated Parmesan Cheese
- ½ cup chopped toasted **PLANTERS** Pecans, divided
- ¼ cup chopped fresh parsley
-    **RITZ** Crackers or **RITZ** Snowflake Crackers

MIX cream cheese, Parmesan cheese and ¼ cup pecans.

SHAPE into 8-inch log. Roll in combined remaining pecans and parsley; press gently into log to secure.

SERVE with crackers.

Makes 12 servings, 2 Tbsp. cheese spread and 5 crackers each.

How to Wrap for Gift-Giving: Place cheese log and small knife on decorative platter or cutting board. Wrap with colorful cellophane and ribbon. After serving the cheese log at the holiday party, the hostess will have a lovely gift to remember the occasion by!

NUTRITION INFORMATION PER SERVING: 190 calories, 15g total fat, 6g saturated fat, 270mg sodium, 12g carbohydrate, 4g protein.

Gift-Giving

NILLA Caramel Popcorn

Prep: 15 min. **Total:** 1 hour 5 min.

- 1 pkg. (14 oz.) **KRAFT** Caramels
- 3 Tbsp. butter or margarine
- 1 Tbsp. water
- 12 cups air-popped popcorn
- 2 cups Mini **NILLA** Wafers

HEAT oven to 300°F. Cook caramels, butter and water in large saucepan on low heat until caramels are melted, stirring frequently.

COMBINE popcorn and wafers in large bowl. Add caramel mixture; toss to coat. Spread onto large greased baking sheet.

BAKE 20 min., stirring after 10 min. Spread onto sheet of waxed paper; cool. Break into clusters.

Makes 18 servings, about 1 cup each.

Use Your Microwave: To melt caramels in the microwave, place caramels, butter and water in large microwaveable bowl. Microwave on HIGH 2½ to 3 min. or until caramels are completely melted when stirred, stirring after each minute.

Substitute: Substitute Mini **OREO** Cookies or Mini **NUTTER BUTTER** Peanut Butter Sandwich Cookies for the mini wafers.

How to Store: Store in tightly covered container at room temperature for up to 2 weeks.

NUTRITION INFORMATION PER SERVING: 160 calories, 6g total fat, 2.5g saturated fat, 115mg sodium, 27g carbohydrate, 2g protein.

Gift-Giving

Cashew Truffle Surprise

Prep: 30 min. **Total:** 2 hours 30 min. (incl. refrigerating)

1½ pkg. (12 squares) **BAKER'S** Semi-Sweet Chocolate

½ cup whipping cream

½ tsp. vanilla

1 can (9.25 oz.) **PLANTERS** Cashew Halves with Pieces, divided

COOK and stir chocolate and cream in saucepan on low heat until chocolate is completely melted. Stir in vanilla. Refrigerate 1 hour or until firm. Meanwhile, reserve 30 cashew halves. Finely chop remaining cashews.

SHAPE chocolate mixture into 30 (1-inch) balls with melon baller or teaspoon. Insert 1 cashew half into center of each ball; reshape ball to enclose cashew. (Balls need not be perfectly round.) Roll in chopped cashews.

PLACE in waxed paper-lined 15×10×1-inch pan. Refrigerate 1 hour or until firm. Store in tightly covered container in refrigerator. Remove from refrigerator 30 min. before serving to soften slightly.

Makes 2½ doz. or 15 servings, 2 truffles each.

NUTRITION INFORMATION PER SERVING: 240 calories, 19g total fat, 8g saturated fat, 40mg sodium, 18g carbohydrate, 5g protein.

Gift-Giving

Special Extra: For a special touch, drizzle truffles with melted BAKER'S White Chocolate after rolling in chopped cashews. Refrigerate as directed.

Sweet Peanut Brittle

Prep: 5 min. **Total:** 50 min. (incl. refrigerating)

---

1 **cup sugar**

½ **cup light corn syrup**

1 **Tbsp. butter**

2 **cups PLANTERS COCKTAIL Peanuts**

1 **tsp. baking soda**

1 **tsp. vanilla**

4 **squares BAKER'S Semi-Sweet Chocolate**

¼ **cup creamy peanut butter**

SPRAY large baking sheet with cooking spray. Microwave sugar and corn syrup in large glass microwaveable bowl on HIGH 5 min. Stir in butter and peanuts. Microwave 3 to 4 min. or until pale golden brown. Stir in baking soda and vanilla. (Mixture will foam.) Spread onto prepared baking sheet. Cool completely. Break into pieces.

MICROWAVE chocolate in 1-cup glass measuring cup on HIGH 1 to 2 min. or until chocolate is melted when stirred. Add peanut butter; stir until melted. Dip half of each candy piece in chocolate mixture; scrape bottom against edge of cup to remove excess chocolate. Place on sheet of foil or waxed paper. Refrigerate 20 min. or until chocolate is firm.

Makes about 1½ lb. or 16 servings.

Hot and Sweet Peanut Brittle: Stir 1 tsp. hot pepper sauce into candy along with the vanilla.

Fun Idea: Use crushed peanut brittle as a topping for ice cream.

NUTRITION INFORMATION PER SERVING: 250 calories, 14g total fat, 3.5g saturated fat, 190mg sodium, 29g carbohydrate, 6g protein.

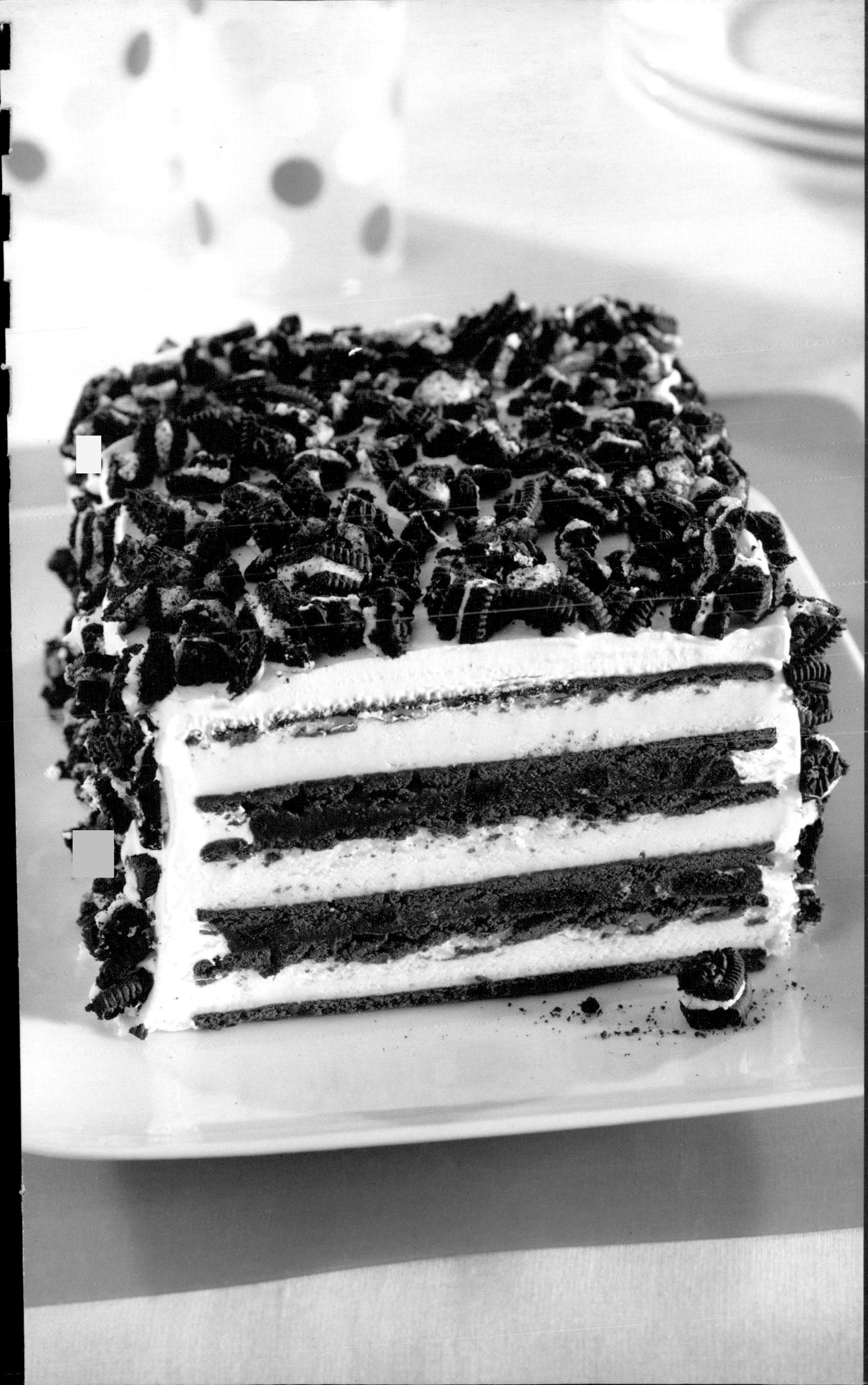

Contents

216

232

274

208

summer's over and the kids are back in school. Along with buses to catch and backpacks to fill, there are all kinds of snacks and desserts to make for after school, classroom parties, holidays, birthdays, and other special occasions. Relax! No matter how busy you are, you've got delicious, easy recipes for all these events right at your fingertips, most requiring less than 30 minutes prep time.

Discover oodles of scrumptious kid-friendly ideas your family can make together. Whip up some **Hot Chocolate-Brownie Cupcakes** and adorable **OREO Frogs** for classroom or party treats. And what child doesn't love **OREO** Cookies with milk? Now you can turn that beloved snack into a cool and creamy **OREO Milk Shake** in just minutes!

Whatever the season, ice cream and frozen desserts are always a hit with the whole family. Keep **CHIPS AHOY! Wiches** on hand in the freezer when you need a quick weeknight dessert. Made with real chocolate chips, **CHIPS AHOY!** Cookies satisfy everyone's love for chocolate. If your dinner guests also enjoy chocolate, indulge their taste buds with decadent **Frozen OREO Fudge-Pop Squares**, the perfect ending to any party.

When you need homemade goodies to bring as gifts or favors, choose from a variety of small bites with big flavor. **Nutty NILLA**

Mallow Bites transform crushed **NILLA** Wafers, cashews, and dried cherries into an irresistible gift-giving confection. Versatile **NILLA** Wafers are used whole or crushed in toppings, crusts, and snack mixes—such as **NILLA-Cinnamon Snack Mix**—so always keep a box on hand for spur-of-the-moment treats. Bring a festive tin of **CHIPS AHOY! Bark** to any gathering and watch everyone's faces light up!

Whether it's a birthday, anniversary, reunion, or a long overdue dinner with friends, all celebrations call for memorable desserts that are extra special, yet simple to make. When everyone breaks open **Molten Chocolate Surprise**, they will be amazed to see a river of chocolate "lava." Only you will know how easy it was to prepare the day beforehand. Decorated like a giant **OREO** Cookie, chocolate-glazed **OREO Celebration Cake** is the ideal go-to cake for any special occasion. Serve no-bake **Chocolate-Caramel Creme Pie** at your next dinner party for a blissful finale sure to please your guests.

Spend a little time making these fabulous treats, and enjoy them with the special people in your life. Start making memories today with *Sweet Treats* from Nabisco.

Marni Leslie
Kraft Kitchens

Kid Favorites

SIMPLE DESSERTS KIDS LOVE

PREP TIME: 20 MINUTES

OREO frogs

2   squares **BAKER'S** Semi-Sweet Chocolate

2   Tbsp. butter or margarine

12   **OREO** Cookies

1/4   cup **JET-PUFFED** Marshmallow Creme

24   miniature pretzel twists

24   candy-coated chocolate pieces

MICROWAVE chocolate and butter in microwaveable bowl on HIGH 1 min. or until chocolate is completely melted and mixture is well blended, stirring every 30 sec.

SPREAD bottom of each cookie with 1 tsp. marshmallow creme, then dip bottom in melted chocolate. Immediately press 2 pretzel twists into chocolate for each frog's legs, with wide part of each pretzel facing outward. Place, pretzel-sides down, on waxed paper-covered baking sheet.

USE remaining melted chocolate to attach candies to tops of cookies for frog's eyes. Let stand until chocolate is firm.

MAKES: 6 servings.

▶ substitute:
Substitute peanut butter for the marshmallow creme.

Nutrition Information Per Serving: 240 calories, 12g total fat, 6g saturated fat, 270mg sodium, 32g carbohydrate, 18g sugars, 2g protein.

183

OREO-apple snack stacks

1 pkg. (8 oz.) **PHILADELPHIA** Cream Cheese, softened

2 Tbsp. honey

$1/2$ tsp. zest and 2 Tbsp. juice from 1 orange, divided

6 **OREO** Cookies, chopped

4 small apples (1 lb.)

4 pretzel sticks

8 worm-shaped chewy fruit snacks

MIX cream cheese, honey and zest in medium bowl until well blended. Stir in chopped cookies. Core apples. Cut each crosswise into 4 rings; brush cut sides with orange juice. Discard any remaining juice.

PAT apple slices dry with paper towels; spread with cream cheese mixture. Restack slices for each apple. Insert pretzel into top of each for the stem.

GARNISH with fruit snacks. Cut horizontally in half to serve.

MAKES: *8 servings.*

make ahead: ◄
Snacks can be made ahead of time. Prepare as directed; wrap with plastic wrap. Refrigerate until ready to serve.

Nutrition Information Per Serving: 210 calories, 11g total fat, 6g saturated fat, 170mg sodium, 25g carbohydrate, 19g sugars, 3g protein.

"cookie dough" ice cream

2 cups vanilla ice cream, softened

8 **CHIPS AHOY!** Cookies, crumbled

MIX ingredients until well blended.

SERVE immediately.

MAKES: 4 servings.

special extra: ◄---
Garnish each serving with an additional
CHIPS AHOY! Cookie, if desired.

Nutrition Information Per Serving: 240 calories,
12g total fat, 6g saturated fat, 135mg sodium,
30g carbohydrate, 22g sugars, 3g protein.

PREP TIME: **5** MINUTES

hot chocolate-brownie cupcakes

30 **CHIPS AHOY!** Cookies, divided

1 pkg. (19 to 21 oz.) brownie mix (13×9-inch pan size)

4 oz. (½ of 8-oz. pkg.) **PHILADELPHIA** Cream Cheese, softened

1 jar (7 oz.) **JET-PUFFED** Marshmallow Creme

1 tsp. vanilla

1 tub (8 oz.) **COOL WHIP** Whipped Topping, thawed

1 tsp. unsweetened cocoa powder

1 cup **JET-PUFFED** Miniature Marshmallows

HEAT oven to 350°F.

SPRAY 24 muffin pan cups with cooking spray. Press 1 cookie onto bottom of each cup. (No problem if cookies crack.) Cut remaining cookies into quarters; set aside.

PREPARE brownie batter as directed on package; spoon into cups. Bake 15 to 18 min. or until toothpick inserted in centers comes out with fudgy crumbs. (Do not overbake.) Cool completely.

BEAT cream cheese, marshmallow creme and vanilla in large bowl with mixer until well blended. Add **COOL WHIP** and cocoa powder; beat just until blended. Spread onto cupcakes; top with marshmallows. Keep refrigerated. Insert 1 cookie piece into side of each cupcake to resemble coffee mug just before serving.

MAKES: 24 servings.

special extra:
Dust with additional cocoa powder just before serving.

Nutrition Information Per Serving: 270 calories, 12g total fat, 4.5g saturated fat, 140mg sodium, 39g carbohydrate, 27g sugars, 2g protein.

188

OREO milk shake

 4 tsp. chocolate syrup

 8 **OREO** Cookies, divided

1¹/₂ cups milk

 2 cups **BREYERS®** All Natural Vanilla Ice
    Cream, softened

SPOON 1 tsp. syrup into each of 4 glasses.
Roll each glass to coat bottom and inside of
glass. Finely chop 4 cookies; set aside.

QUARTER remaining cookies; place in
blender. Add milk and ice cream; blend until
smooth.

POUR into prepared glasses; top with
chopped cookies. Serve immediately.

MAKES: 4 servings, about 1 cup each.

*BREYERS is a registered trademark of Unilever Group
of Companies. © Unilever.*

substitute:
For a lower calorie and fat option, use Reduced Fat
OREO and BREYERS® Smooth & Dreamy™ Fat-Free
Vanilla Ice Cream.

Nutrition Information Per Serving: 300 calories, 13g total
fat, 7g saturated fat, 220mg sodium, 40g carbohydrate,
32g sugars, 6g protein.

easy banana pudding parfaits

- 12 **NILLA** Wafers, divided
- 1/4 cup thawed **COOL WHIP** Whipped Topping, divided
- 1 small banana, cut into 10 slices, divided
- 2 **JELL-O** Vanilla Pudding Snacks

CRUSH 10 wafers to form coarse crumbs; place 1/4 of the crumbs in each of 2 parfait glasses. Top each with 1 Tbsp. **COOL WHIP**, 2 banana slices and half of 1 pudding snack. Repeat layers of crumbs, bananas and pudding.

REFRIGERATE 15 min. Meanwhile, wrap reserved banana slices tightly in plastic wrap; refrigerate until ready to use.

TOP parfaits with remaining **COOL WHIP**, wafers and banana slices just before serving.

MAKES: 2 servings.

how to prevent the banana slices from turning brown: ◄------------------
Toss banana slices with small amount of lemon juice.

Nutrition Information Per Serving: 280 calories, 7g total fat, 4g saturated fat, 290mg sodium, 52g carbohydrate, 34g sugars, 3g protein.

dirt cups

1 pkg. (3.9 oz.) **JELL-O** Chocolate
   Instant Pudding

2 cups cold milk

1 tub (8 oz.) **COOL WHIP** Whipped
   Topping, thawed

15 **OREO** Cookies, finely crushed
   (about 1¼ cups), divided

10 worm-shaped chewy fruit snacks

BEAT pudding mix and milk in large bowl
with whisk 2 min. Let stand 5 min. Stir in
COOL WHIP and ½ cup cookie crumbs.

SPOON into 10 (6- to 7-oz.) paper or
plastic cups; top with remaining cookie
crumbs.

REFRIGERATE 1 hour. Top with fruit snacks
just before serving.

MAKES: 10 servings.

sand cups: ◀
Prepare using JELL-O Vanilla Flavor Instant Pudding
and 35 NILLA Wafers.

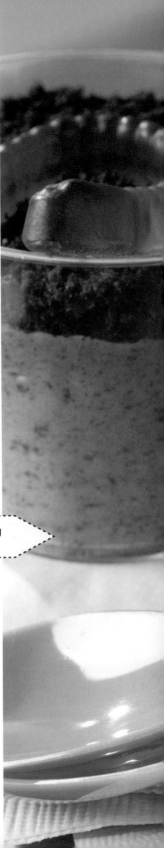

Nutrition Information Per Serving: 230 calories,
9g total fat, 6g saturated fat, 290mg sodium,
36g carbohydrate, 24g sugars, 3g protein.

chewy chips s'more

2 Chewy **CHIPS AHOY!** Real Chocolate Chip Cookies

1 **JET-PUFFED** Marshmallow

PLACE 1 cookie, upside-down, on microwaveable plate; top with marshmallow.

MICROWAVE on HIGH 8 to 10 sec. or until marshmallow puffs.

TOP with second cookie; press down lightly to secure.

MAKES: 1 serving.

substitute: ◄┄┄┄┄┄┄┄┄┄┄┄┄┄┄┄┄┄┄┄┄
Prepare using CHIPS AHOY! Cookies.

Nutrition Information Per Serving: 150 calories, 6g total fat, 3g saturated fat, 85mg sodium, 24g carbohydrate, 15g sugars, 1g protein.

PREP TIME: **5** MINUTES

martians-ate-my-OREO cupcakes

  1 pkg. (2-layer size) chocolate cake mix

  1 pkg. (8 oz.) **PHILADELPHIA** Cream Cheese, softened

  1 egg

  2 Tbsp. sugar

54 Mini **OREO** Cookies, divided

  2 or 3 drops green food coloring

  2 cups thawed **COOL WHIP** Whipped Topping

  4 **OREO** Cookies

¼ cup **JET-PUFFED** Miniature Marshmallows

  4 **JET-PUFFED** Marshmallows, cut in half

  2 pieces string licorice

  1 Tbsp. assorted round candies

HEAT oven to 350°F.

PREPARE cake batter as directed on package. Mix cream cheese, egg and sugar until well blended. Spoon half the cake batter into 24 paper-lined muffin cups. Top each with about 2 tsp. cream cheese mixture and 1 mini cookie; cover with remaining batter.

BAKE 19 to 22 min. or until toothpick inserted in centers comes out clean. Cool 5 min.; remove from pans to wire racks. Cool completely.

STIR green food coloring into **COOL WHIP**; spread onto cupcakes. Split remaining mini and regular-size cookies, leaving all the filling on half of each cookie. Use with remaining ingredients to decorate cupcakes to resemble martians as shown in photo.

MAKES: 2 doz. or 24 servings.

Nutrition Information Per Serving: 250 calories, 15g total fat, 5g saturated fat, 280mg sodium, 28g carbohydrate, 17g sugars, 4g protein.

rocky road
CHIPS AHOY! "pizza"

28 **CHIPS AHOY!** Cookies, divided

$1/4$ cup butter or margarine, melted

4 oz. ($1/2$ of 8-oz. pkg.) **PHILADELPHIA** Cream Cheese, softened

2 Tbsp. powdered sugar

1 cup thawed **COOL WHIP** Whipped Topping

$1/3$ cup **PLANTERS** Cocktail Peanuts, chopped

$2/3$ cup **JET-PUFFED** Miniature Marshmallows

1 square **BAKER'S** Semi-Sweet Chocolate, melted

LINE 9-inch round pan with plastic wrap. Finely crush 24 cookies; mix with butter. Press onto bottom of prepared pan. Chop remaining cookies; set aside.

MIX cream cheese and sugar in medium bowl until well blended. Gently stir in **COOL WHIP**; spread onto crust. Top with nuts, marshmallows and chopped cookies; press lightly into cream cheese layer. Drizzle with chocolate.

REFRIGERATE 1 hour or until firm. Lift pizza from pan using plastic wrap. Remove plastic wrap and cut into slices.

MAKES: 16 servings.

note:
For best results, spray bottom and side of round pan with cooking spray before lining with plastic wrap. This will help the plastic wrap stay in place making it easier to press the cookie crumbs onto bottom of pan.

Nutrition Information Per Serving: 190 calories, 13g total fat, 6g saturated fat, 130mg sodium, 18g carbohydrate, 10g sugars, 2g protein.

OREO baseball dessert

- 1 pkg. (3.9 oz.) **JELL-O** Chocolate Instant Pudding
- 2 cups cold milk
- 35 **OREO** Cookies, divided
- 1¹/₂ cups thawed **COOL WHIP** Whipped Topping
- 1 piece red string licorice (36 inch)

BEAT pudding mix and milk with whisk 2 min. Let stand 5 min. or until thickened.

LINE 8-inch round pan with plastic wrap. Arrange 14 cookies on bottom of pan, cutting to fit if necessary; cover with 1 cup pudding. Repeat layers. Cover with plastic wrap. Refrigerate 24 hours.

UNCOVER dessert. Invert onto serving plate; remove plastic wrap. Frost dessert with **COOL WHIP**. Cut remaining cookies in half; arrange around edge of dessert. Cut licorice into 2 (8-inch) pieces and 20 (1-inch) pieces. Use licorice to decorate top of dessert to resemble a baseball.

MAKES: 10 servings.

how to easily cut cookies in half:

Refrigerate OREO Cookies first for about 15 min. Then, use a serrated knife to cut in half.

Nutrition Information Per Serving: 280 calories, 11g total fat, 5g saturated fat, 400mg sodium, 44g carbohydrate, 27g sugars, 4g protein.

sun-in-a-cloud

1   cup thawed **COOL WHIP LITE** Whipped Topping

1   **JELL-O** Vanilla Pudding Snack

$^{1}/_{2}$ tsp. colored sprinkles

24   **HONEY MAID** Cinnamon Grahams, broken into quarters

USE large spoon to spread **COOL WHIP** onto small plate, indenting center slightly.

FILL center with pudding; top with sprinkles.

INSERT 8 graham pieces into **COOL WHIP**. Serve with remaining grahams.

MAKES: 1$^{1}/_{2}$ cups dip or 12 servings,
2 Tbsp. dip and 8 graham pieces each.

family fun:
This is a great recipe to prepare with the kids!

Nutrition Information Per Serving: 160 calories, 4.5g total fat, 1.5g saturated fat, 200mg sodium, 28g carbohydrate, 10g sugars, 2g protein.

apple-cinnamon bun dip

1 container (6 oz.) vanilla low-fat yogurt

$1/2$ cup applesauce

$1/2$ tsp. lemon zest

$1/2$ tsp. ground cinnamon

2 tsp. caramel ice cream topping

4 **NILLA** Wafers, coarsely crushed

Additional **NILLA** Wafers for dipping

MIX first 4 ingredients until blended. Drizzle with caramel topping; top with wafer crumbs.

REFRIGERATE 15 min. or until chilled.

SERVE as dip with **NILLA** Wafers.

MAKES: 1$1/4$ cups dip or 10 servings, 2 Tbsp. dip and 8 wafers each.

special extra:
For a unique dip container, cut off top and hollow out large red apple. Stand upright on serving platter; fill with dip. Surround with wafers.

Nutrition Information Per Serving: 170 calories, 6g total fat, 1.5g saturated fat, 135mg sodium, 27g carbohydrate, 15g sugars, 2g protein.

strawberry
NILLA nibbles

4 Reduced Fat **NILLA** Wafers

2 Tbsp. thawed **COOL WHIP LITE** Whipped
   Topping

2 fresh strawberries, halved

PLACE wafers on small dessert plate.

TOP with **COOL WHIP** and berries.

MAKES: 1 serving.

substitute: ◄----------------------------------
Prepare using COOL WHIP FREE Whipped Topping.

Nutrition Information Per Serving: 90 calories, 2g total fat,
1.5g saturated fat, 60mg sodium, 17g carbohydrate,
9g sugars, less than 1g protein.

NILLA tic-tac-toe

Tic-Tac-Toe is even more fun when you play it with **NILLA** Wafers! Draw a large Tic-Tac-Toe grid on sheet of paper (or use decorating icing to draw grid). Use icings or gels to write X's on 5 wafers in one color and O's on 5 more wafers in another color. Play as many games as you like, then when you are done you can eat the playing pieces!

OREO 1,2,3's

Playing with numbers can be a real treat when it's done with **OREO** Cookies. Use decorating icings or gels to write one number, from 0 to 9, on each of 10 cookies. Also, write a "minus," "plus" and "equal" sign on 3 more cookies. Use the decorated **OREO** "math" cookies to help your child practice counting from 1 to 10. Then, ask your child to arrange the cookies in numerical order. Use the numbers to create simple math problems and ask your child to solve them.

CHIPS AHOY! a,b,c's

Make spelling fun with the help of **CHIPS AHOY**! Cookies. Use decorating icings or gels to write a different letter of the alphabet on 26 regular or Mini **CHIPS AHOY**! Cookies. Then, use the cookies to have your child practice spelling simple words or names. Or, use the decorated cookies to play a game of **CHIPS AHOY**! Scramble. Just select the appropriate decorated cookies to make a word, scramble the cookies, then ask your child to guess the secret word.

Please see Nutrition Facts panel on packages for serving sizes.

Frozen Treats

FROSTY DELIGHTS THAT PLEASE THE WHOLE FAMILY

PREP TIME: **20** MINUTES

NILLA tortoni "cake"

- 1 pkg. (12 oz.) **NILLA** Wafers (about 88 wafers), coarsely crushed (about 5 cups)
- 1 cup **PLANTERS** Slivered Almonds, toasted
- 1¾ qt. (7 cups) vanilla ice cream, softened
- ½ cup caramel ice cream topping

SPRINKLE 1 cup wafer crumbs and ⅓ cup nuts onto bottom of 9-inch springform pan; cover with half the ice cream. Repeat layers. Top with remaining crumbs and nuts; press into ice cream with back of spoon to secure.

FREEZE 4 hours.

REMOVE side of pan before cutting dessert into wedges to serve. Drizzle with caramel topping.

MAKES: 16 servings.

 how to toast nuts:

Spread nuts into single layer in shallow pan. Bake at 350°F for 5 to 7 min. or until lightly toasted, stirring occasionally.

Nutrition Information Per Serving: 280 calories, 14g total fat, 5g saturated fat, 150mg sodium, 37g carbohydrate, 25g sugars, 5g protein.

OREO & fudge ice cream cake

 ½ cup hot fudge ice cream topping, warmed

 1 tub (8 oz.) **COOL WHIP** Whipped Topping, thawed, divided

 1 pkg. (3.9 oz.) **JELL-O** Chocolate Instant Pudding

16 **OREO** Cookies, chopped (about 2 cups), divided

12 vanilla ice cream sandwiches

POUR fudge topping into medium bowl. Whisk in 1 cup **COOL WHIP**. Add dry pudding mix; stir 2 min. Stir in 1 cup chopped cookies.

ARRANGE 4 ice cream sandwiches, side-by-side, on 24-inch-long piece of foil; top with half the **COOL WHIP** mixture. Repeat layers. Top with remaining sandwiches. Frost top and sides with remaining **COOL WHIP**; press remaining chopped cookies into **COOL WHIP** on top and sides of cake. Bring up foil sides; double fold top and ends to loosely seal packet.

FREEZE 4 hours.

MAKES: 12 servings.

note: ◀
The consistency of fudge topping can vary depending on what brand you purchase. If your fudge topping mixture is too thick to spread easily, stir in up to ¼ cup milk.

Nutrition Information Per Serving: 370 calories, 15g total fat, 9g saturated fat, 410mg sodium, 56g carbohydrate, 32g sugars, 4g protein.

CHIPS AHOY!
wiches

3 cups vanilla ice cream, slightly softened

24 **CHIPS AHOY!** Cookies

3/4 cup sprinkles

SPREAD 1/4 cup ice cream onto flat side of each of 12 cookies. Cover with remaining cookies to make 12 sandwiches.

ROLL edges in sprinkles.

FREEZE 1 to 2 hours or until firm.

MAKES: 1 doz. or 12 servings.

variation:
Prepare using your favorite flavor of ice cream, sherbet or frozen yogurt. In addition, roll edges in chopped PLANTERS Nuts, colored sprinkles, chocolate chips or toasted BAKER'S ANGEL FLAKE Coconut instead of the sprinkles.

Nutrition Information Per Serving: 220 calories, 9g total fat, 4g saturated fat, 105mg sodium, 35g carbohydrate, 26g sugars, 2g protein.

216

PREP TIME: 20 MINUTES

frozen lemonade squares

9   **HONEY MAID** Low Fat Honey Grahams, finely crushed (about 1¼ cups)

⅓   cup margarine or butter, melted

4   cups frozen vanilla yogurt, softened

6   oz. (½ of 12-oz. can) frozen lemonade concentrate, thawed

½   cup thawed **COOL WHIP LITE** Whipped Topping

MIX graham crumbs and margarine; press onto bottom of 9-inch square pan.

BEAT yogurt and concentrate with mixer until well blended; spread over crust.

FREEZE 4 hours or until firm. Serve topped with **COOL WHIP**.

MAKES: 9 servings.

special extra: ◄-------------------------------
Garnish with fresh mint sprigs and lemon slices or peel.

Nutrition Information Per Serving: 250 calories, 11g total fat, 3g saturated fat, 210mg sodium, 36g carbohydrate, 23g sugars, 3g protein.

NILLA yogurt freeze

2 Reduced Fat **NILLA** Wafers

2 Tbsp. thawed **COOL WHIP LITE** Whipped Topping

2 Tbsp. strawberry low-fat yogurt

PLACE 1 wafer in paper-lined medium muffin cup; cover with combined **COOL WHIP** and yogurt.

TOP with remaining wafer.

FREEZE 1 hour or until firm.

MAKES: 1 serving.

substitute: ◄---

Prepare using your favorite flavor of yogurt.

Nutrition Information Per Serving: 80 calories, 2g total fat, 1.5g saturated fat, 45mg sodium, 14g carbohydrate, 9g sugars, 1g protein.

221

cherry-vanilla ice cream pie

18 **OREO** Cookies, finely crushed
   (about 1¹/₂ cups)

3 Tbsp. butter or margarine, melted

3 cups vanilla ice cream, softened

1 can (21 oz.) cherry pie filling,
   divided

1 Tbsp. chocolate syrup

COMBINE cookie crumbs and butter;
press onto bottom and up side of 9-inch
pie plate sprayed with cooking spray.
Refrigerate until ready to use.

MIX ice cream and 1¹/₂ cups pie filling;
spoon into crust. Freeze 4 hours or until
firm.

DRIZZLE chocolate syrup over pie. Serve
topped with remaining cherry pie filling.

MAKES: 10 servings.

substitute:

Prepare using a chocolate syrup that hardens to
form a "shell" when drizzled over the pie.

Nutrition Information Per Serving: 280 calories,
12g total fat, 6g saturated fat, 180mg sodium,
41g carbohydrate, 30g sugars, 3g protein.

CHIPS AHOY!
ice cream cake

    1   pkg. (15.25 oz.) **CHIPS AHOY!** Cookies (39 cookies), divided
    1/4 cup butter or margarine, melted
    3/4 cup hot fudge ice cream topping, divided
    3   cups vanilla ice cream, divided
    3   cups chocolate ice cream, divided
    3/4 cup thawed **COOL WHIP** Whipped Topping
    7   maraschino cherries

SET aside 12 cookies. Crush remaining cookies; mix with butter. Press 2/3 onto bottom of 9-inch springform pan. Stand reserved cookies around edge. Microwave 1/2 cup fudge topping as directed on package; drizzle over crust. Freeze 15 min.

SOFTEN 1 1/2 cups of <u>each</u> flavor ice cream; spread, 1 flavor at a time, over fudge layer in crust. Sprinkle with remaining crumb mixture. Scoop remaining ice cream into balls; place over crumb layer.

FREEZE 4 hours or until firm. When ready to serve, top dessert with **COOL WHIP**. Microwave remaining fudge topping as directed on package; drizzle over dessert. Garnish with cherries.

MAKES: 12 servings.

note: ◄
If you don't have a springform pan, you can prepare dessert in 9-inch pie plate instead.

Nutrition Information Per Serving: 440 calories, 23g total fat, 11g saturated fat, 260mg sodium, 56g carbohydrate, 36g sugars, 5g protein.

OREO cookies & creme pudding pops

1 pkg. (3.4 oz.) **JELL-O** Vanilla Flavor Instant Pudding

2 cups cold milk

12 **OREO** Cookies, divided

$\frac{1}{2}$ cup thawed **COOL WHIP** Whipped Topping

BEAT pudding mix and milk in medium bowl with whisk 2 min.

CHOP 6 cookies; crush remaining cookies. Spoon half the crushed cookies onto bottoms of 10 (3-oz.) paper or plastic cups.

ADD chopped cookies and **COOL WHIP** to pudding; stir just until blended.

SPOON pudding mixture into cups; top with remaining crushed cookies. Insert wooden pop stick or plastic spoon into each for handle. Freeze 5 hours or until firm.

MAKES: 10 servings.

how to remove frozen pops from cups:

Hold frozen cups with hands on sides of cups to warm pops slightly before removing from cups. To remove pops, press firmly onto bottom of cup to release pop. Do not twist or pull pop stick.

Nutrition Information Per Serving: 130 calories, 4.5g total fat, 2g saturated fat, 230mg sodium, 22g carbohydrate, 16g sugars, 2g protein.

frozen OREO
fudge-pop squares

- 5 squares **BAKER'S** Semi-Sweet Chocolate, divided
- 18 **OREO** Cookies, crushed (about 1²/₃ cups)
- 3 Tbsp. butter or margarine, melted
- 2 tubs (8 oz. each) **PHILADELPHIA** Cream Cheese Spread
- 1 can (14 oz.) sweetened condensed milk
- 1 cup thawed **COOL WHIP** Whipped Topping

LINE 9-inch square pan with foil, with ends of foil extending over sides. Melt 4 chocolate squares as directed on package; set aside. Mix cookie crumbs and butter; press onto bottom of prepared pan.

BEAT cream cheese spread in large bowl with mixer until creamy. Gradually beat in milk. Blend in melted chocolate. Whisk in **COOL WHIP**. Spoon over crust. Freeze 6 hours. Meanwhile, make curls from remaining chocolate square.

REMOVE dessert from freezer 15 min. before serving. Top with chocolate curls. Use foil handles to lift dessert from pan.

MAKES: 16 servings.

how to make chocolate curls:

Warm a square of BAKER'S Baking Chocolate by microwaving it, unwrapped, on HIGH for a few seconds or just until you can smudge the chocolate with your thumb. Hold the square steadily and draw a peeler slowly over flat bottom of square, allowing a thin layer of chocolate to curl as it is peeled off the bottom of the square to make long, delicate curls. Use the same technique along the narrow side of the square to make short curls.

Nutrition Information Per Serving: 290 calories, 18g total fat, 11g saturated fat, 240mg sodium, 30g carbohydrate, 25g sugars, 4g protein.

Gift-Giving Classics

DECORATIVE CANDIES, MUFFINS, AND SMALL BITES THAT ARE PERFECT FOR GIVING

PREP TIME: 20 MINUTES

CHIPS AHOY! turtles

3 squares **BAKER'S** Semi-Sweet Chocolate, divided

1 Tbsp. butter or margarine

12 **CHIPS AHOY!** Cookies

6 **KRAFT** Caramels

2 tsp. milk

12 **PLANTERS** Pecan Halves

MICROWAVE 2 chocolate squares and butter in microwaveable bowl on HIGH 1 min. or until chocolate is melted and mixture is well blended, stirring every 30 sec. Spread onto tops of cookies. Let stand 15 min. or until chocolate is firm.

MICROWAVE caramels and milk in small microwaveable bowl on HIGH 1 min.; stir until smooth. Melt remaining chocolate square as directed on package.

SPOON caramel onto centers of cookies; top with nuts. Drizzle with melted chocolate. Let stand 30 min.

MAKES: 1 doz. or 12 servings.

▶ gift-giving:
To give as a gift, pack several cookie turtles in decorative container or tin lined with colorful plastic wrap or tissue paper.

Nutrition Information Per Serving: 120 calories, 7g total fat, 3g saturated fat, 60mg sodium, 15g carbohydrate, 9g sugars, 1g protein.

OREO chocolate-raspberry truffle cups

1/4 cup butter or margarine, divided

12 **OREO** Cookies, finely crushed (about 1 cup)

2 Tbsp. raspberry jam

1 pkg. (6 squares) **BAKER'S** White Chocolate

1/2 cup whipping cream, divided

6 squares **BAKER'S** Semi-Sweet Chocolate

2 Tbsp. white or multi-colored sprinkles

MELT 2 Tbsp. butter; mix with cookie crumbs. Press onto bottoms of 24 miniature paper-lined muffin cups. Add 1/4 tsp. jam to each. Refrigerate until ready to use.

MICROWAVE white chocolate, 1/4 cup cream and 1 Tbsp. of the remaining butter in microwaveable bowl on HIGH 1 min.; stir until chocolate is melted and mixture is well blended. Spoon over jam. Freeze 10 min.

MEANWHILE, melt semi-sweet chocolate with remaining cream and butter as directed for white chocolate. Spoon over white chocolate layer; top with sprinkles. Refrigerate 1 to 2 hours or until firm.

MAKES: 2 doz. or 24 servings.

substitute: ◄-----

For variety, substitute marshmallow creme, peanut butter, caramel sauce or a different flavor of jam for the raspberry jam in the recipe.

Nutrition Information Per Serving: 140 calories, 9g total fat, 5g saturated fat, 50mg sodium, 15g carbohydrate, 12g sugars, 1g protein.

nutty NILLA
mallow bites

3 Tbsp. butter or margarine

1 pkg. (10½-oz.) **JET-PUFFED** Miniature
   Marshmallows (about 6 cups)

1 pkg. (12 oz.) **NILLA** Wafers, coarsely crushed
   (about 5 cups)

1 cup **PLANTERS** Cashews, chopped

½ cup dried cherries, chopped

LINE 13×9-inch pan with foil, with ends of foil
extending over sides; spray with cooking spray.

MICROWAVE butter in large microwaveable bowl on
HIGH 45 sec. or until melted. Add marshmallows; toss
to coat. Microwave 1½ min. or until marshmallows
are completely melted and mixture is well blended,
stirring every 45 sec.

ADD remaining ingredients; mix well. Press onto
bottom of prepared pan; cool. Use foil handles to lift
dessert from pan; cut into 1-inch squares.

MAKES: 8 doz. or 24 servings, 4 squares each.

gift-giving: ◀--

These bite-size treats make perfect gifts for family and friends.
Place in paper candy cups or mini cupcake liners, then pack in
a holiday gift box for a one-of-a-kind gift.

Nutrition Information Per Serving: 160 calories, 7g total fat,
2g saturated fat, 100mg sodium, 23g carbohydrate, 14g sugars,
2g protein.

double-chocolate OREO fudge

   6 cups sugar, divided
1 1/2 cups butter or margarine, divided
   2 small cans (5 oz. each) evaporated milk (about 2/3 cup each)
1 1/2 pkg. (12 squares) **BAKER'S** Semi-Sweet Chocolate
   2 jars (7 oz. each) **JET-PUFFED** Marshmallow Creme, divided
   1 cup chopped **PLANTERS** Macadamias
   2 tsp. vanilla, divided
   2 pkg. (6 squares each) **BAKER'S** White Chocolate
   8 **OREO** Cookies, chopped

LINE 13×9-inch pan with foil, with ends of foil extending over sides. Place 3 cups sugar, 3/4 cup butter and 1 can evaporated milk in 3-qt. heavy saucepan. Bring to full rolling boil on medium heat, stirring constantly. Cook 4 min. or until candy thermometer reaches 234°F, stirring constantly. Remove from heat.

ADD semi-sweet chocolate and 1 jar marshmallow creme; stir until melted. Add nuts and 1 tsp. vanilla; mix well. Pour into prepared pan; spread to cover bottom of pan.

BRING remaining sugar, butter and evaporated milk to full rolling boil in separate 3-qt. heavy saucepan on medium heat, stirring constantly. Cook 4 min. or until candy thermometer reaches 234°F, stirring constantly. Remove from heat.

ADD white chocolate and remaining marshmallow creme; stir until melted. Stir in chopped cookies and remaining vanilla. Pour over chocolate layer in pan; spread to evenly cover. Cool at room temperature 4 hours before cutting into pieces. Store in tightly covered container at room temperature.

MAKES: 6 1/4 lb. or 72 servings, 1 piece each.

cooking know-how: ◄-------------------------------
If you don't have a candy thermometer, bring sugar mixture to full rolling boil on medium heat, then begin timing 4 min. while mixture continues to boil, stirring constantly.

Nutrition Information Per Serving: 190 calories, 9g total fat, 4.5g saturated fat, 50mg sodium, 28g carbohydrate, 26g sugars, 1g protein.

NILLA-cinnamon snack mix

3 cups **NILLA** Wafers

1 cup **PLANTERS** Pecan Halves

1 cup pretzel sticks

3 Tbsp. butter or margarine, melted

2 Tbsp. sugar

1 tsp. ground cinnamon

$1/4$ tsp. kosher salt

$1/2$ cup yogurt-covered raisins

HEAT oven to 375°F.

COMBINE first 3 ingredients in large bowl. Mix butter, sugar, cinnamon and salt. Drizzle over wafer mixture; toss to coat.

SPREAD onto bottom of foil-lined 15×10×1-inch pan.

BAKE 10 min. or until lightly toasted, stirring after 5 min. Cool. Stir in raisins.

MAKES: 6 cups or 24 servings, $1/4$ cup each.

how to store: ◄
Store in airtight container at room temperature.

Nutrition Information Per Serving: 150 calories, 9g total fat, 2.5g saturated fat, 125mg sodium, 17g carbohydrate, 9g sugars, 1g protein.

banana-nut graham muffins

16 **HONEY MAID** Honey Grahams, finely crushed (about 2²/₃ cups)

¹/₄ cup sugar

2 tsp. **CALUMET** Baking Powder

1 egg

1 cup fat-free milk

2 Tbsp. honey

2 fully ripe bananas, mashed

¹/₄ cup chopped **PLANTERS** Walnuts

HEAT oven to 400°F.

COMBINE graham crumbs, sugar and baking powder until well blended. Mix all remaining ingredients except nuts in large bowl. Add graham mixture; stir just until moistened.

SPOON into 12 paper-lined muffin cups; top with nuts.

BAKE 15 to 18 min. or until toothpick inserted in centers comes out clean. Cool in pan 5 min. Remove to wire rack; cool slightly.

MAKES: 1 doz. or 12 servings.

substitute: ◄- -

Substitute semi-sweet chocolate chips for the nuts.

Nutrition Information Per Serving: 160 calories, 4.5g total fat, 1g saturated fat, 220mg sodium, 29g carbohydrate, 16g sugars, 3g protein.

CHIPS AHOY! bark

1 pkg. (8 squares) **BAKER'S** Semi-Sweet Chocolate, chopped

1 pkg. (6 squares) **BAKER'S** White Chocolate, chopped

10 **CHIPS AHOY!** Cookies, coarsely broken, divided

1/4 cup dried cranberries, divided

MICROWAVE semi-sweet and white chocolates in separate medium microwaveable bowls as directed on package. Stir 1/3 cup cookies and 1 Tbsp. cranberries into chocolate in each bowl.

DROP spoonfuls of the 2 chocolate mixtures alternately onto waxed paper-covered baking sheet; swirl gently with knife. Sprinkle with remaining cookies and cranberries.

REFRIGERATE 1 hour or until firm. Break into pieces.

MAKES: 14 servings.

special extra: ◄ -

Toast 1/4 cup PLANTERS Slivered Almonds. Add 1 Tbsp. nuts to melted chocolate in each bowl before dropping onto baking sheet and swirling as directed. Sprinkle with remaining nuts, cookies and cranberries.

Nutrition Information Per Serving: 190 calories, 11g total fat, 6g saturated fat, 35mg sodium, 24g carbohydrate, 19g sugars, 2g protein.

graham break-aways

12 **HONEY MAID** Honey Grahams, broken in half (24 squares)

$1/2$ cup butter or margarine

$3/4$ cup packed brown sugar

1 cup **BAKER'S** Semi-Sweet Chocolate Chunks

$1/2$ cup finely chopped **PLANTERS** Pecans

HEAT oven to 350°F.

ARRANGE graham squares in single layer in 15×10×1-inch pan.

BRING butter and sugar to boil in medium saucepan on medium heat; cook 2 min. or until butter is completely melted and mixture is well blended, stirring frequently. Pour over grahams; immediately spread to completely cover grahams.

BAKE 6 to 8 min. or until topping is hot and bubbly. Top with chocolate; bake 1 to 2 min. or until melted. Immediately spread chocolate over grahams. Sprinkle with nuts; press lightly into chocolate with back of spoon. Cool completely before breaking into squares.

MAKES: 24 servings.

almond-white chocolate graham break-aways:

Prepare as directed, substituting PLANTERS Slivered Almonds for the pecans and 6 squares BAKER'S White Chocolate, chopped, for the semi-sweet chocolate chunks.

Nutrition Information Per Serving: 140 calories, 9g total fat, 4g saturated fat, 80mg sodium, 17g carbohydrate, 12g sugars, 1g protein.

PREP TIME: 15 MINUTES

Sweet Celebrations

DESSERT CREATIONS
FOR ALL OCCASIONS

PREP TIME: 10 MINUTES

cookie "fun-due"

1 pkg. (8 squares) **BAKER'S** Semi-Sweet Chocolate

1 cup whipping cream

CHIPS AHOY! Cookies

MICROWAVE chocolate and whipping cream in large microwaveable bowl on HIGH 2 min. or until chocolate is completely melted and mixture is well blended, stirring after each minute.

SERVE warm with **CHIPS AHOY**! Cookies for dipping.

MAKES: 1³/₄ cups or 14 servings, 2 Tbsp. dip and 3 cookies each.

▶ special extra:
Serve with additional dippers, such as OREO Cookies, OREO CAKESTERS Soft Snack Cakes, NILLA Wafers, HONEY MAID Graham Crackers, JET-PUFFED Marshmallows, strawberries, banana chunks and apple slices.

Nutrition Information Per Serving: 290 calories, 19g total fat, 9g saturated fat, 120mg sodium, 32g carbohydrate, 18g sugars, 3g protein.

mini OREO cheesecakes

44	**OREO** Cookies, divided
3	pkg. (8 oz. each) **PHILADELPHIA** Cream Cheese, softened
³/₄	cup sugar
³/₄	cup **BREAKSTONE'S** or **KNUDSEN** Sour Cream
1	tsp. vanilla
3	eggs
2	squares **BAKER'S** White Chocolate, melted
¹/₂	cup colored sprinkles
1¹/₂	cups thawed **COOL WHIP** Whipped Topping

HEAT oven to 325°F.

PLACE 1 cookie in each of 24 paper- or foil-lined muffin pan cups. Chop 8 of the remaining cookies; set aside.

BEAT cream cheese and sugar with mixer until blended. Add sour cream and vanilla; mix well. Add eggs, 1 at a time, beating after each just until blended. Gently stir in chopped cookies. Spoon into baking cups.

BAKE 18 to 20 min. or until centers are set. Cool completely. Refrigerate 3 hours or until chilled. Meanwhile, cut remaining cookies in half. Dip cookie halves halfway in melted chocolate. Place on waxed paper-covered baking sheet; top with sprinkles. Let stand 15 min. or until chocolate is firm.

TOP each cheesecake with dollop of **COOL WHIP** and cookie half just before serving.

MAKES: 2 doz. or 24 servings.

make ahead:
Cheesecakes can be stored in refrigerator up to 3 days, or frozen up to 1 month, before topping with COOL WHIP and cookie half just before serving. If freezing cheesecakes, thaw overnight in refrigerator before garnishing.

Nutrition Information Per Serving: 280 calories, 17g total fat, 9g saturated fat, 230mg sodium, 29g carbohydrate, 21g sugars, 4g protein.

peanut butter cup squares

25 **NUTTER BUTTER** Cookies, divided

$^1/_4$ cup butter or margarine, melted

1 pkg. (8 oz.) **PHILADELPHIA** Cream Cheese, softened

$^1/_2$ cup creamy peanut butter

1 cup cold milk

1 pkg. (3.4 oz.) **JELL-O** Vanilla Flavor Instant Pudding

$2^1/_2$ cups thawed **COOL WHIP** Whipped Topping, divided

3 squares **BAKER'S** Semi-Sweet Chocolate

LINE 9-inch square pan with foil, with ends of foil extending over sides. Finely crush 24 cookies. Mix with butter; press onto bottom of prepared pan.

BEAT cream cheese and peanut butter in medium bowl with whisk until well blended. Add milk and dry pudding mix; beat 2 min. Stir in 1 cup **COOL WHIP**; spoon over crust. Refrigerate until ready to use.

MICROWAVE remaining **COOL WHIP** and chocolate in microwaveable bowl on HIGH $1^1/_2$ to 2 min. or until chocolate is completely melted and mixture is well blended, stirring after each minute. Cool completely.

SPREAD chocolate mixture over pudding layer in pan. Chop remaining cookie; sprinkle over chocolate mixture. Refrigerate 4 hours or until firm. Use foil handles to lift dessert from pan before cutting to serve.

MAKES: 16 servings.

PREP TIME: 15 MINUTES

s'mores dessert squares

64	**NILLA** Wafers, divided
5	Tbsp. butter or margarine, melted
3	Tbsp. sugar
1	pkg. (3.9 oz.) **JELL-O** Chocolate Instant Pudding
3¼	cups cold milk, divided
2	pkg. (3.4 oz. each) **JELL-O** White Chocolate Flavor Instant Pudding
1½	cups thawed **COOL WHIP** Whipped Topping
1½	cups **JET-PUFFED** Miniature Marshmallows
½	square **BAKER'S** Semi-Sweet Chocolate, grated

HEAT oven to 350°F.

CRUSH 40 wafers finely; place in medium bowl. Add butter and sugar; mix well. Press onto bottom of 13×9-inch pan. Bake 8 min. or until lightly browned. Cool.

BEAT 1 pkg. chocolate pudding mix and 1¼ cups milk with whisk 2 min.; spread over crust. Cover with remaining wafers. Beat white chocolate pudding mixes and remaining milk in medium bowl with whisk 2 min. Stir in **COOL WHIP**. Spread over wafer layer in pan. Refrigerate 3 hours or until firm.

HEAT broiler just before serving dessert. Top dessert with marshmallows; broil, 6 inches from heat, 1 min. or until marshmallows are puffed and lightly browned. Sprinkle with grated chocolate.

MAKES: 24 servings.

take along:
Assemble dessert in 13×9-inch disposable foil pan. Wrap tightly in plastic wrap and refrigerate as directed. Store in an insulated cooler packed with plenty of ice or frozen gel packs to take along to your party destination. Uncover and top with marshmallows just before serving, then broil as directed.

Nutrition Information Per Serving: 160 calories, 6g total fat, 3.5g saturated fat, 260mg sodium, 27g carbohydrate, 19g sugars, 2g protein.

tropical strawberry cream pie

42 **NILLA** Wafers, divided

3 Tbsp. butter or margarine, melted

1 pkg. (8 oz.) **PHILADELPHIA** Cream Cheese, softened

1/4 cup sugar

2 cups thawed **COOL WHIP** Whipped Topping, divided

1 can (8 oz.) crushed pineapple, drained

3/4 cup boiling water

1 pkg. (3 oz.) **JELL-O** Strawberry Flavor Gelatin

1 cup ice cubes

2 cups sliced strawberries

CRUSH 26 wafers; mix with butter until well blended. Press onto bottom of 9-inch pie plate. Stand remaining wafers around edge of pie plate.

BEAT cream cheese and sugar in large bowl with mixer until well blended. Gently stir in 1 cup **COOL WHIP** and pineapple; spread over crust.

ADD boiling water to gelatin mix in medium bowl; stir 2 min. until completely dissolved. Stir in ice until melted. Add strawberries; stir. Refrigerate 5 min. or until slightly thickened; spoon over cream cheese layer. Refrigerate 4 hours or until set. Top with remaining **COOL WHIP,** if desired.

MAKES: 8 servings.

Nutrition Information Per Serving: 370 calories, 21g total fat, 13g saturated fat, 260mg sodium, 41g carbohydrate, 31g sugars, 4g protein.

chocolate-caramel creme pie

4	oz. ($^{1}/_{2}$ of 8-oz. pkg.) **PHILADELPHIA** Cream Cheese, softened
2	Tbsp. caramel ice cream topping
1	cup thawed **COOL WHIP** Whipped Topping
1	**OREO** Pie Crust (recipe follows)
1	pkg. (3.9 oz.) **JELL-O** Chocolate Instant Pudding
1$^{1}/_{2}$	cups cold milk

MIX cream cheese and caramel topping in medium bowl until well blended. Gently stir in **COOL WHIP**; spread onto bottom of **OREO** Pie Crust.

BEAT pudding mix and milk with whisk 2 min.; pour over cream cheese layer. Refrigerate 3 hours.

MAKES: 8 servings.

Nutrition Information Per Serving: 310 calories, 17g total fat, 10g saturated fat, 460mg sodium, 38g carbohydrate, 25g sugars, 4g protein.

OREO PIE CRUST

PREP: 15 min. TOTAL: 15 min.

18	**OREO** Cookies
3	Tbsp. butter or margarine, melted

PLACE cookies in large resealable plastic bag; press bag to remove excess air, then seal bag. Use rolling pin to crush cookies to form fine crumbs.

ADD butter; squeeze bag to evenly moisten crumbs.

PRESS crumb mixture onto bottom and up side of 9-inch pie plate sprayed with cooking spray. Refrigerate until ready to fill.

MAKES: 1 (9-inch) crust, 8 servings.

Nutrition Information Per Serving: 150 calories, 9g total fat, 4.5g saturated fat, 160mg sodium, 18g carbohydrate, 10g sugars, 1g protein.

how to easily serve crumb-crust pies:

When serving a crumb-crust pie, dip filled pie plate in warm water for 10 sec., being careful to dip pie plate to just below rim. This will help loosen the crust to make it easier to serve the cut pieces.

molten chocolate surprise

- 4 squares **BAKER'S** Semi-Sweet Chocolate
- 1/2 cup butter or margarine
- 2 whole eggs
- 2 egg yolks
- 1 cup powdered sugar
- 1/3 cup flour
- 12 **CHIPS AHOY!** Cookies
- 1/2 cup thawed **COOL WHIP** Whipped Topping

HEAT oven to 425°F.

MICROWAVE chocolate and butter in large microwaveable bowl on HIGH 2 min. or until butter is melted. Stir until chocolate is completely melted. Beat whole eggs, yolks, sugar and flour with whisk until well blended. Gradually beat into chocolate mixture.

LINE 12 muffin pan cups with paper liners; spray with cooking spray. Place 1 cookie, upside-down, on bottom of each cup; cover with batter.

BAKE 8 min. or until cakes are firm around edges but still soft in centers. Cool in pan 1 min. Carefully remove cakes from pan. Invert into dessert dishes; remove paper liners. Serve with **COOL WHIP**.

MAKES: 1 doz. or 12 servings.

make ahead:
Batter can be prepared ahead of time. Cover and refrigerate up to 24 hours. When ready to serve, pour batter evenly over cookies in prepared muffin cups and bake as directed.

Nutrition Information Per Serving: 240 calories, 15g total fat, 9g saturated fat, 105mg sodium, 26g carbohydrate, 18g sugars, 3g protein.

OREO celebration cake

2 Tbsp. unsweetened cocoa powder	1 cup water
20 **OREO** Cookies, divided	1/2 cup **BREAKSTONE'S** or **KNUDSEN** Sour Cream
1 1/2 cups flour	2 squares **BAKER'S** Semi-Sweet Chocolate, melted
1 tsp. **CALUMET** Baking Powder	2 1/2 tsp. vanilla, divided
1 tsp. baking soda	1 pkg. (16 oz.) powdered sugar, divided
2 eggs, separated	3 Tbsp. milk
1 cup granulated sugar	Chocolate Glaze (recipe follows)
2/3 cup butter or margarine, softened, divided	

HEAT oven to 350°F.

SPRAY 2 (9-inch) round pans with cooking spray; dust with cocoa powder. Coarsely chop 7 cookies. Finely crush remaining cookies; place in medium bowl. Add flour, baking powder and soda; mix well.

BEAT egg whites with mixer on high speed until stiff peaks form; set aside. Beat granulated sugar, 1/3 cup butter and egg yolks with mixer until well blended. Add flour mixture, water, sour cream, melted chocolate and 1 tsp. vanilla; beat on medium speed 1 min. Gently stir in egg whites until well blended. Pour into prepared pans.

BAKE 25 min. or until toothpick inserted in centers comes out clean. Cool in pans 10 min. Remove to wire racks; cool completely.

BEAT 1 cup powdered sugar with remaining butter and vanilla in large bowl with mixer until well blended. Add remaining powdered sugar alternately with milk, beating well after each addition. Reserve 1/2 cup frosting.

PLACE 1 cake layer on plate; spread with remaining frosting. Sprinkle with chopped cookies; top with remaining cake layer. Spread top with Chocolate Glaze. Let stand 10 min. Decorate with reserved frosting. Keep refrigerated.

MAKES: 16 servings.

Nutrition Information Per Serving: 410 calories, 17g total fat, 9g saturated fat, 260mg sodium, 67g carbohydrate, 49g sugars, 4g protein.

PREP TIME: 25 MINUTES

CHOCOLATE GLAZE

PREP: 5 min. TOTAL: 10 min.

4 squares **BAKER'S** Semi-Sweet Chocolate

1 Tbsp. butter or margarine

MICROWAVE chocolate and butter in microwaveable bowl on HIGH 1 min. or until chocolate is melted and mixture is well blended, stirring every 30 sec.

MAKES: ¹/₂ cup or 8 servings, 1 Tbsp. each.

Nutrition Information Per Serving: 80 calories, 6g total fat, 3.5g saturated fat, 10mg sodium, 8g carbohydrate, 6g sugars, less than 1g protein.

eggnog eclair dessert

1 pkg. (8 oz.) **PHILADELPHIA** Cream Cheese, softened

2 cups cold milk

1 pkg. (3.4 oz.) **JELL-O** Vanilla Flavor Instant Pudding

1/2 tsp. rum extract

1/4 tsp. ground nutmeg

1 tub (8 oz.) **COOL WHIP** Whipped Topping, thawed, divided

78 **NILLA** Wafers

2 squares **BAKER'S** Semi-Sweet Chocolate

BEAT cream cheese in large bowl with mixer until creamy. Gradually beat in milk. Add dry pudding mix, extract and nutmeg; beat 2 min. Gently stir in 1 1/2 cups **COOL WHIP**.

LINE 9×5-inch loaf pan with plastic wrap. Arrange 15 wafers, top-sides down, on bottom of pan; cover with 1/4 of the pudding mixture. Repeat layers 3 times. Top with 15 of the remaining wafers. Refrigerate 3 hours.

INVERT dessert onto plate; remove plastic wrap. Microwave chocolate and 1 cup of the remaining **COOL WHIP** in microwaveable bowl on HIGH 25 sec.; stir until chocolate is completely melted and mixture is well blended. Cool 1 min. Pour over dessert. Garnish with remaining **COOL WHIP** and wafers.

MAKES: 12 servings.

variation: ◄

Omit rum extract and substitute eggnog for the milk.

Nutrition Information Per Serving: 300 calories, 17g total fat, 10g saturated fat, 300mg sodium, 35g carbohydrate, 23g sugars, 4g protein.

262

PREP TIME: 30 MINUTES

tiramisu bowl: serve it your way!

1 pkg. (8 oz.) **PHILADELPHIA** Cream Cheese, softened

3 cups cold milk

2 pkg. (3.4 oz. each) **JELL-O** Vanilla Flavor Instant Pudding

1 tub (8 oz.) **COOL WHIP** Whipped Topping, thawed, divided

48 **NILLA** Wafers

1/2 cup brewed strong **MAXWELL HOUSE** Coffee, cooled

2 squares **BAKER'S** Semi-Sweet Chocolate, coarsely grated

1 cup fresh raspberries

FOR THE FILLING:

BEAT cream cheese in large bowl with mixer until creamy. Gradually beat in milk and dry pudding mixes. Gently stir in 2 cups **COOL WHIP**.

NOW, YOU CHOOSE!

BOWL: Line bottom and side of 2½-qt. bowl with half the wafers; drizzle with half the coffee. Top with half the pudding mixture and chocolate. Repeat layers. Top with remaining **COOL WHIP** and raspberries. Refrigerate 3 hours.

PAN: Line bottom of 13×9-inch pan with half the wafers; drizzle with half the coffee. Top with half the pudding mixture and chocolate. Repeat layers. Top with remaining **COOL WHIP** and raspberries. Refrigerate 3 hours.

PARFAITS: Place 1 wafer on bottom of each of 16 dessert dishes; drizzle each with 3/4 tsp. coffee. Top each with 1/4 cup pudding mixture and a sprinkle of chocolate. Add layers of remaining wafers and pudding; top with remaining chocolate, **COOL WHIP** and raspberries. Refrigerate 3 hours.

MAKES: 16 servings, about 2/3 cup each.

Nutrition Information Per Serving: 230 calories, 12g total fat, 7g saturated fat, 300mg sodium, 29g carbohydrate, 20g sugars, 3g protein.

googly eyes

White decorating icing

2 **OREO CAKESTERS** Soft Snack Cakes

2 cinnamon red hot candies

Red decorating gel

PLACE large dot of white decorating icing near edge of each snack cake.

PRESS 1 candy into icing to resemble eyeball.

USE red decorating gel to add squiggly lines for the veins.

MAKES: 1 serving.

substitute: ◄---------------------------------
Substitute candy-coated chocolate pieces for the cinnamon candies.

Nutrition Information Per Serving: 260 calories, 12g total fat, 2.5g saturated fat, 250mg sodium, 38g carbohydrate, 26g sugars, 2g protein.

PREP TIME: 5 MINUTES

INDEX